PRAISE FOR THE ART AND BUSINESS OF SPEECH RECOGNITION

"Blade Kotelly's delightful book provides a well-grounded and highly readable introduction to creating automated dialogue systems using speech recognition. Kotelly takes his extensive experience and training and distills it for beginning speech designers and their managers. He rightfully reminds us that there is art in designing any successful product. The technology only makes the product possible; it doesn't make it usable.

The Art and Business of Speech Recognition brings us key concepts in voice user interface and application design—concepts critical to making the system acceptable to a user. Yet Kotelly does so in a way that makes those concepts easy to absorb, with many examples from real applications. Page after page produces the "Aha!" that makes an important principle stick.

Anyone who has responsibility for a system that will conduct an automated speech dialogue with the public should read this book. The public will be well served."

—WILLIAM MEISEL
PRESIDENT, TMA ASSOCIATES
PUBLISHER/EDITOR, *SPEECH RECOGNITION UPDATE* NEWSLETTER

"Forget the technology, and don't even think about protocols, until you read this book! Usability is what drives the ROI on speech systems, and Blade takes you there. **You can buy this book and save yourself and your company a bundle of time and money, or pay the price later.** Blade has designed some of the biggest systems out there, and he's put it all in this book. Grab on to his experience before you start writing your first app!"

—MARK PLAKIAS
SENIOR VICE PRESIDENT, COMMUNICATIONS & INFRASTRUCTURE
THE KELSEY GROUP

"This book is as engaging and enjoyable as the interfaces it enables designers to create. Based on theoretical studies of communication and on Kotelly's long experience as a virtuoso voice interface designer, it provides a clear step-by-step introduction to the art of designing and implementing an effective and satisfying user experience."

—TERRY WINOGRAD
PROFESSOR, STANFORD UNIVERSITY, AND COAUTHOR OF
BRINGING DESIGN TO SOFTWARE AND *UNDERSTANDING COMPUTERS AND COGNITION*

"This book explains why good design is essential not only to achieve more fully the traditional goal of automated phone systems—automating more calls—but to seize the huge opportunity today to create an enjoyable experience—one that actually delights customers. **Blade knows the subtleties of designing an effective speech service and provides the reader with an appreciation for the importance of those fine points.**"

—WILLIAM SCHWARTZ
SENIOR VICE PRESIDENT, VOICE RESPONSE UNIT DESIGN
BANK OF AMERICA

"Blade Kotelly's *The Art and Business of Speech Recognition* is an engaging and accessible introduction to how to design a "noble" speech application. Kotelly takes on the role of the caller advocate, and takes the reader through the caller's mind in a speech-user experience, showing

* How to maximize the efficiency of the experience

* How to entice the user to speak in a way that the system can comprehend

* How to walk the fine line between appealing anthropomorphism and efficient automation

* How to provide subtle pointers to educate the caller without appearing condescending

In this book, Kotelly also gives good advice to businesses considering speech implementation. He convincingly illustrates that a telephony speech interface is much more than a "better touch-tone." He shows that speech offers better return on investment, and even more importantly, speech adds a "human touch." This "human touch" appeals to the caller's emotion, and projects an image that is helpful, forgiving, engaging, and even fun. The "human touch" also offers a fantastic opportunity to strengthen branding and connect to the customer. Kotelly's sound business advice extends to measuring ROI, usability, caller satisfaction, and uncovering "bugs" in the system. **This book is a must-read for anyone thinking about designing speech interfaces or deploying speech applications.**"

—KAI-FU LEE
CORPORATE VICE PRESIDENT
NATURAL INTERACTIVE SERVICES DIVISION
MICROSOFT CORPORATION

THE ART AND BUSINESS
OF SPEECH RECOGNITION

THE ART AND BUSINESS OF

SPEECH RECOGNITION

CREATING THE NOBLE VOICE

BLADE KOTELLY

✦ Addison-Wesley

Boston • San Francisco • New York • Toronto • Montreal
London • Munich • Paris • Madrid
Capetown • Sydney • Tokyo • Singapore • Mexico City

The publisher offers discounts on this book when ordered in quantity for bulk purchases and special sales. For more information, please contact:

U.S. Corporate and Government Sales
(800) 382-3419
corpsales@pearsontechgroup.com

For sales outside of the U.S., please contact:

International Sales
(317) 581-3793
international@pearsontechgroup.com

Visit Addison-Wesley on the Web: www.awprofessional.com

Library of Congress Cataloging-in-Publication Data
Kotelly, Blade.
    The art and business of speech recognition : creating the noble voice / Blade Kotelly.
        p. cm.
    Includes index.
    ISBN 0-321-15492-4 (alk. paper)
    1. Automatic speech recognition. I. Title.

TK7882.S65.K635 2003
384.6'4—dc21

2002028332

ISBN 0-321-15492-4
Text printed on recycled paper
1 2 3 4 5 6 7 8 9 10—CRS—0706050403
First printing, January 2003

This book is totally and completely dedicated to my mom and dad.

CONTENTS

Speech-recognition technology increasingly is being used in a variety of over-the-phone applications in the transportation, financial, telecommunications, and other industries. Most people by now have experienced at least one automated phone system, where questions are posed by a computer to callers seeking help or information, and the callers' spoken answers are understood and acted on by that computer. In the best cases, the computer even sounds human!

Given the rapid emergence of these applications, the time seems right for a concise overview of the topic—a guide for business managers looking for new and better ways to engage and service their customers, a resource for designers getting started with voice applications (or refreshing their current knowledge), a good read for anyone interested in this exciting technology. Having built applications in many of these industries, I feel well-positioned, and eager, to explain important aspects of the art and business of speech recognition, and to illuminate the extraordinary returns a well-designed and well-deployed over-the-phone system can yield—increased revenues, lower costs, customer satisfaction and retention, and brand development. Speech-recognition technology can give a company an identifiable and welcome voice—a noble voice, even—and in this book I mean to show how.

The key to voice-application success, as I demonstrate in a variety of examples, is a well-constructed user interface—interactions between the system and its users that are both pleasing and effective. The best voice interfaces avoid the confusion or annoyance of touchtone systems and the expense of operators or customer representatives. A good voice interface, as the examples will illustrate, can solve critical business problems.

This book certainly is not meant to be exhaustive in its coverage of speech-recognition technology, or to be academically rigorous in its style. Other fine books delve more deeply and exclusively into particular elements of design, such as brainstorming techniques and usability testing principles. Rather, this book is the product of one experienced, business-focused practitioner—me—talking about what works in this domain, and what does not. I speak from the real-world perspective of a designer who has had to fight with deadlines, work around technological limitations, satisfy and excite the system's users, all while meeting contractual obligations to the client and financial expectations. (That experience will sound familiar to *all* practitioners!) From this perspective, I convey insights and advice about user-interface design, production, testing, and deployment that I hope will help others plan and build their own successful speech-recognition applications.

Readers familiar with other software development processes will see some similarities between the design of systems for over-the-phone speech-recognition systems and the design of systems for other media. This book, however, focuses on that which is unique to designing speech-recognition systems. It is important for client companies and designers alike to understand these unique elements in order to produce a system that works optimally for both the client company and its calling population.

To keep the book's focus on more fundamental design concepts, I have chosen not to discuss specific technologies, algorithms, or programming methodologies that may be popular at the moment, but that likely will change with each passing year, or perhaps even soon become obsolete. Thus, I do not cover VoiceXML, SSML, and certain proprietary software packages currently in use; although important and popular today, these changing standards are less central for understanding the basic principles.

There are two principal audiences for this book.

- People who want to be effective speech-recognition user-interface designers

- People who want to understand or profit from these systems

Prospective designers should find all chapters of the book useful. Other readers—particularly call center managers, programmers/implementers, and project managers—are likely to benefit most from the chapters that address the design and deployment process, and the ideas that drive the process (Chapters 5, 6, 7, 9, and 10).

After you've read this book, you will have a fundamental understanding of what goes into the design, production, testing, and deployment of over-the-phone speech-recognition applications. You'll have learned design guidelines, tips, and techniques that help ensure an application will work well and that people will enjoy using it. Inasmuch as examples are often the best way to learn, you'll have seen how other designers have dealt with real-life issues to solve real business problems. By addressing the main principles behind the creation of speech-recognition systems, I hope to have shown you the tight connection between the process of solving business problems using speech-recognition technology and the art of designing those systems.

PHILOSOPHY

No matter how immersed they become in the minutiae, designers of over-the-phone speech-recognition systems must never lose sight of one, over-arching goal: These systems are made to *help* people do what they *have* to do. It doesn't matter if it's mundane (home banking) or flashy (entertainment/infotainment like a voice-portal), the goal is the same: to help people accomplish their tasks swiftly, easily, and unobtrusively.

Every designer should be guided by a philosophy. Having a philosophy gives a designer both a starting position and a compass to point the way—a compass to navigate through the plethora of decisions that must be made along the way. At the very least, having a philosophy enables a designer to answer the "*Why?*" question at each point in the design process. Why am I writing this question? Why am I using a particular word here in a particular context? Why will *this* design solve the problem better than another design?

When I was about four years old, my mom taught me that if I was confused at all about whether or not to do something, I could simply think about the Golden Rule: "Do unto others as you would have them do unto you." Her point was to make sure that I considered other people's perspectives before I did something that might affect them. I've applied this rule both consciously and subconsciously throughout my life in a variety of situations.

When I was a teenager, I became driven by the idea that I should design things—at that point I wasn't sure just what things—that improved people's lives. Eventually, this winding road led me to become a speech-recognition system designer. And when I first approached problems and thought about how to develop the best solutions, I wandered back to the Golden Rule as a way to solve design problems on a variety of levels. I've found that this rule is especially applicable in the design of speech-recognition systems.

When designing a system, designers need to put themselves mentally in the place of the people calling into the system. If we can understand what it's like to be those people in their varying moods—happy, angry, confused, rushed, or impatient—we can design a system to accommodate them. While empathizing is not always easy to do, we can often satisfy callers by understanding who they are and why they're calling, and then decide on the most appropriate way to handle different callers and different situations. Some situations are easy to design for, while others present problems that require more work to solve. In both cases knowledge of *psychology* will aid the designer more than knowledge of *technology* alone.

ACKNOWLEDGMENTS

Special thanks to the following people for their time reviewing, editing, and contributing to this work: Deanne Harper, James Cassidy, Dan Faulkner, Harry Hersh. Thanks, too, to those without whom this work would not have been possible, whose mentorship and education have changed the way that I (and I'm sure countless others) see the world: Dr. John Kreifeldt, Timothy "Lucky" Lawlor, Tony Lovell, Jon Mann, Dr. Salvatore Soracci, Gerald Taylor, Dr. Judith Wechsler, Penn Young. Thanks to my colleagues and fellow designers: Mike Ahnemann, Todd Chapin, Peter Crimmin, Jose Elizondo, Phil Farhi, Dr. Jason Humphries, Marie McCarthy, Erik van der Neut, Derek Seabury, Jan Smith, Steve Springer. Thanks to the production staff at Addison-Wesley for all their expertise in producing this: Amy Fleischer, Peter Gordon, Rebecca Greenberg, Karin Hansen, Curt Johnson, Hartley Ferguson, Richard Oriolo, Rob Mauhar, and Northwind Editorial Services. Thanks to the following people for their generous support: Steve Chambers, Mark Holthouse, Stuart Patterson, Charlie Rutledge, Richard Westelman.

PART I

THE BACKGROUND

In recent years large companies have started to use speech-recognition technology to serve their customers better, save money, and even grow revenue. However, the technology alone doesn't enable these benefits—effective speech-recognition user-interface design is critical to achieve these goals.

Many companies are confronted with the question: How can we satisfy thousands (or millions) of customers who, for the most part, all want the same information? To answer this question, we think about using automation technologies and self-service technologies. Connect a database to a Web server, add a good user interface, and millions of people who have computers can get information they need. However, not everyone has access to a computer when they want or need to use one. And some problems or questions are still best handled by a live customer-service representative. The telephone is a logical technology to take advantage of, since telephones and cellular phones are ubiquitous.

One solution that takes advantage of the phone as a medium for self-service is the call center. Hire lots of people to answer phones, train them correctly, and provide them access to the right information. Once again we solve a business problem, but unfortunately time has shown us that call centers are often poorly staffed by representatives who may or may not represent the company well to a caller who may have had to wait for several minutes, only to be talking to the wrong person. In this all-too-common case, the problems are not solved—they are exacerbated, and with this solution the company does not get any cost-savings associated with self-service automation.

So how can we satisfy thousands or millions of customers who need or want to use the telephone to interact with the company? Touchtone systems have been used to solve this problem, but are infamous for their caller-satisfaction catastrophes that result from poor design and technological limitations. Speech-recognition technology can overcome many of the technological limitations associated with touch-tone systems, but must be used the right way, for the right customers to solve the right business problems.

Part I of this book is a primer that covers why businesses have chosen to deploy speech recognition, the basic principles of the recognition technology, and the psychological aspects that underlie all speech-recognition applications. It is important to consider how each of these three elements are inexorably related: the business problems can only be solved using robust technology; however, understanding and using the best technology doesn't mean that callers will want to use the deployed system or will be able to use it. A system that fulfills all the objectives can only be rendered if the designer has an understanding of social psychology and how to apply it.

ONE

ON TELEPHONES, TOUCHTONES,
AND BUSINESS NEEDS

Speech is power: speech is to persuade, to convert, to compel.
—RALPH WALDO EMERSON

There are three things in speech that ought to be considered before some things are spoken—the manner, the place and the time.
—ROBERT SOUTHEY

Social-psychological research has shown that people treat media the same way as they treat other people. The moment a speech-recognition system answers and asks a caller a question, the speech system becomes a social actor.[1] This interaction between computer and human will influence the way each caller feels about that developing relationship. And it is through this constructed, human-machine dialogue that the company has the opportunity to create its "Noble Voice": a single voice to handle all issues with elegance, all complaints with genuine concern, and to treat all people—regardless of race, sex, age, perceived intelligence, or accent—equally. A voice to serve 24 hours a day, 365 days a

---

1. Byron Reeves and Clifford Nass, *The Media Equation: How People Treat Computers, Television, and New Media Like Real People and Places* (New York: Cambridge University Press, 1996).

year, requiring no vacation or time off. A voice, that when it fails to aid the caller with their task, can still treat them elegantly, and with egalitarian politeness.

To construct this Noble Voice in a way to provide callers with a positive experience, we have to understand some of the underlying aspects of society, technology, communication, and commerce.

The telephone has become indispensable for both personal and business communication. It's easy to understand why. The telephone offers an immediacy that's essential in today's world; it is extraordinarily intuitive and easy to use; and as the cost of long-distance calling has dropped and wireless technology has proliferated, it has never been more accessible.

For the first 65 years after Alexander Graham Bell invented the telephone in 1876, people could only communicate over the phone with other people. With the development of touchtone systems in 1941 by Bell System, we gained the ability to communicate over the phone with computers by pressing keys on the telephone keypad. By the 1970s many companies had begun to use this technology to automate aspects of their call centers. More recently, speech-recognition software has enabled us to interact with computers using only our voices. **Speech recognition** is a technology that enables a computer to identify and act upon what a person has said. And unlike personal computer speech-recognition software, which typically is used by a single person to dictate letters to a computer, telephony-based speech-recognition software enables thousands of people, simultaneously, to use any cellular or landline phone to contact a company and have a simple conversation about a particular subject. With telephone-based speech recognition systems customers can contact companies to retrieve flight information, book tickets for events, and even trade stocks over the phone.

Many companies now use the phone to market their brand identities, sell more products and services to their existing customers, and provide customers with access to information when they're traveling. People can call their bank and get immediate, up-to-date checking account and credit-card balance information without having to talk to someone. As voice and data networks converge, the range of services that can be delivered over the phone continues to grow. An increasing number of companies deliver their services over the phone at low cost, 24 hours a day, 7 days a week, every day of the year using automation techniques. The increasing sophistication of speech-recognition technology, coupled with the universal appeal of the telephone, has opened up a new world of business opportunities for companies of all kinds.

According to Epoch Partners, Inc. and International Data Corporation (IDC), companies made Customer Relationship Management (CRM) a $6.6 billion business in 2000 as they integrated their call centers, corporate databases, and computer systems into a coherent whole to attract and retain customers. To achieve the full potential of CRM, companies need to fully leverage the power of the telephone. With that power, they can better retain the loyalty of their existing customers, reach new customers, generate advertising revenue, save money, and better support and build their brands. Touchtone systems achieve *some* of these objectives. Speech-recognition technology can be used to achieve *all* of them.

SPEECH RECOGNITION VERSUS TOUCHTONE FUNCTIONALITY

Speech recognition helps companies overcome the limitations of touchtone systems, which are often difficult to use for anything other than the most rudimentary applications. Nearly all of us have had at least one experience of being trapped in touchtone menu hell—unable to accomplish tasks or escape, except by hanging up. The frustration caused by these experiences often leads to customer disenchantment and ill will. As a result, many companies have found themselves needing to support unsuccessful touchtone systems by hiring additional—and costly—call center representatives, negating one of the motivations for purchasing a touchtone system in the first place.

Unlike impersonal touchtone systems, speech-recognition systems give companies a greater power to bond with their customers. Not only does the nature of conversational interaction enable a more natural experience for the caller than a touchtone system, but speech-recognition systems can also make some complex tasks easier to automate, thereby reducing the cost of handling routine matters. Imagine what it would be like if the customer service representatives at United Airlines had to personally answer thousands of calls each day from people seeking basic flight departure and arrival information. It is unrealistic to expect even the best customer representative to treat a caller with the same high level of courtesy and respect that he showed the previous 1,000 callers that day. But with a well-designed speech-recognition system, a company can treat every one of its customers as if the very best representative was serving them—promptly, efficiently, helpfully, and unobtrusively.

Is there anything touchtone can do that speech recognition cannot? The short answer is no, but there are occasions when many people will prefer to use touchtone. People rather like that touchtone allows them to enter a Personal Identification Number (PIN) in relative secrecy (rather than saying it out loud, possibly in front of strangers). However, if they're in a private setting where no one can hear them, they may very well choose to speak.

It is often a good idea to combine speech and touchtone to give callers a choice, as when a system says, "Enter or say your phone number." Some people prefer to use touchtone systems to enter numerical data because it's a kinesthetic process they've grown accustomed to after years of using touchtone telephones and automated teller machines. Many people have a better kinesthetic memory for phone numbers; we need to run our hands over a touchtone keypad to recall the correct sequence of numbers.

But speech-recognition is a better modality for many other tasks, including ones that have traditionally been viewed as numeric. For example, I recently used a touchtone system to get credit for an incorrect long-distance charge. The touchtone system gave me the following directions in a rather slow and laborious manner:

> "To request credit using this system, I will ask you to use your telephone to enter the amount to be credited to your bill in dollars and cents. You must enter numbers for the cents, even if they are zeros, but you do not have to enter a decimal point. For example, for a credit of two dollars and thirty-five cents, you would enter *two, three, five*. For a credit of three dollars, you would enter *three, zero, zero*. Or for a credit of nine cents, you would enter *zero, nine*."

A speech-recognition system would handle the same task by simply asking, "How much was the charge?" The caller could very naturally reply, "Twenty-six cents" or "Three dollars and fifteen cents" without any further instructions needed.

Given the functional and business attractions of using speech technology, you would expect that it would be widely deployed. While many more touchtone systems exist, there are a significant number of speech-recognition applications on the market today. The top providers of telephone-based speech-recognition solutions boast over hundreds of deployments they've done themselves, and over thousands of deployments of their technology by their various partners in the years between 1997 and 2002.[2]

PROBLEMS WITH TOUCHTONE, AND A SPEECH RECOGNITION REMEDY

You often hear people complaining about a touchtone system they've used. Sometimes the technology is implemented in such a way that it confuses or angers callers. And since companies typically use these systems as the front line of telephone communication, customers may be forced to endure a poorly designed system that may *aid the company* in cost-reduction but *may frustrate the caller*. Other times the technology is being used for a task that it doesn't serve well.

Movie theater information systems are a common touchtone application, and they illustrate the limitations of the technology. Here's how a popular one works.

When filmgoers call in, the application welcomes them and asks them to press "1" if they know the name of the film they want to see, and "2" if they want to browse all films currently showing.

Callers who press "1" are asked to enter the first three letters of the film's title. This is where things get dicey. The application goes on to tell callers that if the first word of the title has fewer than three letters or if any of those first three letters is "Q" or "Z," they should press "1" again. Callers who press "1" then have to listen to the entire list of current films and press yet another key when they hear the one they want. By this point some callers are probably thinking that they could have walked to the corner newsstand, bought the daily paper, and checked the film schedule in less time.

2. Data from marketing material by Nuance Communications, Inc. and SpeechWorks International, Inc.

There is nothing catastrophically wrong with this touchtone interaction. It may give people the information they need—it's just that touchtone isn't very well suited to the job at hand. The application forces callers to accommodate its limitations—the fact that each button represents more than one letter and the lack of "q" and "z" on most telephone keypads—rather than making things as easy as possible for them.

A speech-recognition system's ability to ask a direct question and then act on the response enables a much more efficient transaction. What if we tackled the movie information interaction described above with speech-recognition technology? The application would simply say to callers:

"If you know which film you'd like to see, say its name."

The speech-recognition solution is more elegant, more intuitive, and much faster because the user provides the information in a completely natural way. There is no need to learn how to use the system, no need to hear redundant information, and no need to explicitly decline listening to redundant information. With that one concise prompt, the speech-recognition method can handle every caller need after option "1" in the touchtone application.

Speech-recognition systems can also tailor the calling experience to the needs of the user, offering more detailed assistance as needed to novice or infrequent callers—and ultra-fast, streamlined service to more experienced callers. Even if a failure occurs, the system can resolve the problem elegantly and optimally, because every facet has been designed and crafted for clarity and comprehension at every moment of the conversation.

When a company implements a speech-recognition system, it can take greater advantage of its phone lines to handle customers' needs while satisfying the needs of the company. With a well-designed system, a company can present a single, consistent personality to the customer, instead of the several—or even several hundred—personalities of its call center representatives. During the design process, that personality can be precisely tailored to reinforce the company's brand identity and marketing strategy. Speech-recognition systems can also provide a very high quality experience for the consumer, an impact that cannot be overstated.

A well-designed system doesn't just solve business problems or simply adhere to the company's branding strategy—it can also create a strong connection between the system and the caller, a connection that is felt viscerally. Deeply. One person who reviewed a system I worked on, reflecting on her experience said, "By the end of using this system, you'll want to take the voice to dinner."[3] All it did was provide flight arrival and departure information!

Speech-recognition technology is constantly improving, too. Today's speech-recognition systems can understand more than just one word or phrase at a time. If a system asks a caller, "OK, what's your travel itinerary?" and the caller responds, "Boston to San Diego, tomorrow at 3 P.M.," chances are good that the system will understand what was spoken. In fact, a typical North American English speech-recognition system is so good that it can match a single spoken utterance against a list of 80,000 items with upwards of 95% accuracy while still being able to respond to the caller with the next question or statement in tenths of a second.

WHAT KINDS OF COMPANIES ARE USING SPEECH RECOGNITION?

United Airlines has several speech-recognition systems, including employee travel reservations, consumer flight information, up-to-the-minute reporting of lost baggage, and other applications for frequent flyers. American Airlines, AirTran Airways, and Continental Airlines also have speech-recognition systems for flight information.

Then there are companies, such as FedEx and United Parcel Service (UPS), that use speech recognition to help people track packages. FedEx also uses a speech-recognition system to provide shipping cost estimates over the phone.

A number of companies in the financial services industry use speech-recognition systems both to provide information and to enable customers to conduct transactions. They include E*TRADE, Charles Schwab, Wachovia, Bank of America, and Fidelity Investments.

---

3. Julie Vallone, *Investor's Business Daily*, December 23, 1999.

Text-to-speech (TTS) technology, which enables computers to read text to callers, is being used in conjunction with speech-recognition systems so that Yahoo! and America Online users can listen to their e-mail messages from any telephone. Other companies use TTS to provide consumers with a weather-band radio—the ability to hear up-to-the-minute, local weather reports provided by the National Weather Service in all of the United States, adjacent coastal waters, Puerto Rico, the U.S. Virgin Islands, and the U.S. Pacific Territories—being spoken by a computer.

For an entire new breed of companies, speech recognition is not a service enabler, but the service itself. Among them are **voice portals**—the telephone equivalent of Web portals—that provide information on weather, stocks, driving directions, movie listings, and much more. These include companies such as HeyAnita, Tellme, and BeVocal.

Finally, we can't forget the telephone companies that use speech-recognition technology, including AT&T, Sprint PCS, Verizon, and Singapore Telecommunications (SingTel). Each of these companies uses speech-recognition technology in a variety of ways, from simple call routing to providing information by way of voice portals.

WHY ARE COMPANIES USING IT?

Some companies use speech technology because their customers have been less than satisfied with previous touchtone systems and because speech-recognition systems can solve problems that were previously impossible to solve with touchtone technology. Speech technology also works well, can pay for itself very quickly, and helps to build stronger customer relationships. For example, in the first 30 months after United Airlines deployed their speech-recognition flight information system, the system had handled over 50 million calls, and United Airlines had saved over $24 million. The system paid for itself within the first few months of deployment and has been lauded as one of the best uses of speech-recognition design.

In June of 2002, the Kelsey Group's Voice and Wireless Commerce research team conducted a study of nine speech-recognition applications that had been deployed by SpeechWorks International. On average, the annual savings per deployment was $1.02 million, with an average return on investment reached in 9 months. When the company was replacing a touchtone system, the *increase* in automation was between a low of 30% and a high of 55%. One company commented that after implementing a speech-recognition solution in place of a touchtone system, the abandonment rate of callers dropped by 50%.

SPEECH-RECOGNITION APPLICATIONS: A TYPICAL EXAMPLE

Before we get into the particulars of the design process, let's examine what a typical speech-recognition application looks like. Here's an example of a person calling the AirTran flight information toll-free number. The following exchange ensues.

SYSTEM: Welcome to the AirTran Airways Flight Information System. If you've never called before, say "Instructions." Do you know the flight number?

CALLER: *Yes.*

SYSTEM: OK. What is it?

CALLER: *Three forty-one.*

SYSTEM: Thanks. Do you want arrival or departure information?

CALLER: *Departure.*

SYSTEM: Is it departing Saturday, Sunday, or Monday?

CALLER: *Sunday.*

SYSTEM: Great. Hold on while I check on that flight. Here it is. Flight three forty-one departed on time from Boston, Massachusetts at 6:40 A.M. and is scheduled to arrive on time in Atlanta, Georgia at 9:00 A.M. on September 23rd. Please check for specific gate information at the airport. You can say, "Repeat that," "Check another flight," or "Good-bye."

CALLER: *Good-bye.*

SYSTEM: Thanks for calling AirTran Airways. Good-bye.

Let's examine some elements of this conversation.

When the system answers the telephone call, it plays an **audio file**, a recorded, spoken prompt. The caller then responds. At this and each succeeding **turn** (also called a **state**—in a speech-recognition application where the system asks the caller a question and then listens for an answer), the system analyzes the sound of what it has heard to determine whether or not it was something it expected to hear. So, for example, when the system asks the caller for "arrival or departure information," it is expecting to hear "Arrival" or "Departure" or even similar phrases, such as "Arrival information" or "Departure information."

However, when it asks for the flight number, it's expecting to hear one of many, many different responses. For example, the caller might say, "Three twenty-one," "Three, two, one," "Flight three twenty-one," "Flight three, two, one," or any other number within a particular range of a few thousand possible flight numbers. Because of this, speech-recognition systems have to be designed and tested to ensure that they can "understand" virtually all possible responses that callers to the system are likely to make. That's why the effectiveness of a speech-recognition system can depend greatly on the capabilities of its core technology—the speech recognizer and the way it is used.

WHERE WE'VE BEEN—WHERE WE'RE GOING

The power of speech-recognition technology enables designers to help people in new ways. And similarly to how the underlying principles of design don't change, the same is true about the underlying mechanics of how a speech recognizer functions.

Throughout this book we will make references to the **recognizer**, the technology that enables a system to recognize spoken words. Although system designers needn't become experts on technology to do their jobs well, it's important that they know enough about the workings of the recognizer to understand what it can and cannot do.

TECHNOLOGY PRIMER: ABOUT
SPEECH RECOGNIZERS

Port de bras is the foundation of the great science of the use of arms in classical ballet. The arms, legs and body are developed separately through special
exercises. But only the ability to find the proper position for her arms lends a
finesse to the artistic expression of the dancer, and renders full harmony to
her dance.

—AGRIPPINA VAGANOVA

A speech recognizer listens to people say something, and then attempts to match what
they've said against a list of known (or expected) words or phrases. It sounds simple, but
consider the size of the challenge. In an over-the-phone speech-recognition system, we're
talking about a single computer that has to listen to as many as 48 or 96 people talking
simultaneously over low-fidelity telephone microphones. All of these are people with a
variety of regional accents, people who often don't enunciate clearly, people expecting a
seemingly immediate response. The speech recognizer must process all these data quickly enough to respond accurately and make the interactions feel like natural conversations.

It's clearly a daunting task, which is why all over-the-phone speech-recognition systems use a kind of electronic shorthand. Instead of listening and trying to understand

every word a person might say, they listen for a small set of key words—as few as two and as many as several hundred thousand, depending on the system and its constraints.

Take, for example, when a speech-recognition system asks callers to say their U. S. ZIP code numbers. It can expect to hear a series of any five out of a possible ten digits (zero to nine) in response, as well as "oh" for "zero." Because the vocabulary of the responses is constrained to a fixed-length string of just five digits (no letters), algorithms enable the computer to quickly figure out the ZIP code spoken by each caller. On the other hand, if the system had to listen to bank account numbers—which often vary in length (certain companies have account numbers that can be anywhere between 8 and 16 digits) and may include letters and dashes in addition to the numbers—it would have a harder time breaking down the sounds due to the lack of constraints on the length of the string and the wider scope of valid utterances.

The more the system designer can constrain the vocabulary for each response, the greater the speed and accuracy of the speech recognition. That's why most over-the-phone speech systems collect street addresses by first asking for the ZIP codes: the system dynamically loads only the list of valid streets for that area, then when it asks for the street name (or street address) it can match the caller's utterance against the limited list of street names in that ZIP code. If the system were to ask a caller for the street address first (in the way that people do to each other), and a caller said "1221 Gray Street," the system would have to match this against a significantly larger list of possible street names—compromising the speed and accuracy of the recognition.

Designers have to be prepared to make trade-offs between sounding natural ("What's your street address?") and ensuring accuracy ("In which ZIP code is that address located?"). And because the capabilities of speech recognizers vary greatly, designers also have to consider the strengths or limitations of their speech recognizer as they design an application.

There are several different recognizers available today, each of which has its own strengths and weaknesses. Designers need to know how to take advantage of the strengths while working around the weaknesses. While all recognizers listen to spoken utterances and attempt to understand them, many recognizers do other things as well. For example, some recognizers perform **speaker verification**—a security technology that matches a caller's voiceprint to an utterance recorded earlier. While this is a great way to reduce unauthorized use, it is not yet 100% accurate. Therefore, designers must supplement it with other methods of authentication.

Some (but not all) recognizers report statistics that can later be used to analyze the performance of the application. If a system asks, "Where are you flying from?" the recognizer can report many things, some of which include the percentage of times the recognizer needed to ask a question to confirm that it correctly understood what the caller said, as well as the number of callers that hung up the phone after listening to that question. If the recognizer provides more reports, it's generally easier to diagnose problems, as in a case where statistics provided by the recognizer indicate 10% of calls are being transferred to an operator.

Good recognizers provide a method to analyze the data so that the reason(s) for the transfers can be determined. For example, are the transfers all occurring in one state where the caller is asked a particular question? Spread over several states uniformly or randomly? After the application attempts to query a database? Or are the transfers due to callers' requests? And while these statistics don't necessarily indicate the reason for the transfer they do help to point the developer in the right direction.

Also, it is worth noting that some recognizers are **speaker dependent** and require users to train the recognizer for *their* particular voice (generally used on personal computers for dictation applications), while other recognizers are **speaker independent** and can be used by almost anyone, without any training on the part of the caller. The speaker-independent recognizer is by far the most common recognizer for large-scale, telephony-based systems.

WHAT THE RECOGNIZER HEARS (AND THE NEED FOR CONFIRMATION)

Telephone audio quality poses additional challenges. Conventional telephone microphones do not capture the full frequency range of spoken language. They often cut off the higher frequency sounds, such as much of the sound produced when someone says the letter *s*. Furthermore, every time someone speaks into a telephone microphone, the signal is compressed and transmitted across the telephone network, inevitably losing quality along the way. And these days, more people are speaking into tiny microphones on wireless phones in noisy environments and with less than crystal clear reception and transmission. By the time the signal gets to the computer, there's not much left resembling the original utterance. The recognizer has to interpret what the caller is saying using the very limited data that it receives, a job that can be difficult even for people to do well.

We've all become accustomed to listening to voices on the phone and figuring out what people are saying even when a cell phone connection drops seconds of a call. Still, we often confirm information on the phone with each other when it is important to be accurate ("OK, so we're going to meet at eight o'clock at Radius on High Street, right?"). We even may confirm details when talking to someone face-to-face due to the potential for someone hearing something incorrectly. Similarly, speech-recognition systems often confirm things with callers to ensure that it correctly understood what was said.

Confirmation is also used to minimize ambiguity and imprecision. American English is full of homonyms and words with multiple meanings, which can create ambiguity. Take the word "mean," for example. According to the *Oxford English Dictionary*, that word has a total of 21 meanings—7 as a verb, 11 as an adjective, and 3 as a noun. Multiple meanings and homonyms are a challenge for computers—which is why word-processing spelling and grammar checkers often miss mistakes obvious to a human. Add these issues to the ambiguities of the language and the imprecision of colloquial speech, and it's amazing that speech-recognition systems work at all!

For example, say a large software/hardware company uses a speech-recognition system to answer help desk calls and solve basic problems. Imagine that the system has great speech-recognition technology, understands a very large vocabulary of technical terms, and can recognize many types of questions. Here's how a typical call might go.

SYSTEM: **Welcome to the MegaComp help desk line. How may I help you?**
CALLER: *Uh, I'm having a networking problem with my new software and server.*

Despite all its advanced capabilities, the computer would still have to ask clarifying questions because of the ambiguity and imprecision of spoken language.

In this example the caller could mean

* There's a problem between the new software and an existing server.

* There's a problem between the new software and a new server.

* There's a problem on the network as a result of installing new software and a new server.

* There's a problem on the network as a result of installing new software on an existing server.

* There's a problem on the network as a result of installing new software, and there's a separate, unrelated problem with the server.

Designers have to take all of these possible meanings into account and structure the application accordingly. By writing prompts carefully and inserting confirmations at any point where callers provide critical information, designers can ensure a more efficient, friendly, and accurate system.

WHEN THE RECOGNIZER LISTENS

It's not only *what* the recognizer hears that can pose a challenge, it's also *when* it listens. Computers—like people—need to know when to start listening and when to stop listening.

Have you ever had someone start talking to you when you were deep in thought? You probably missed some of what they initially said. That's because you weren't prepared to start listening. Likewise, sometimes when you cut off someone who is speaking before he or she finishes a thought, you might miss some important piece of information. Sensing when to start and stop talking in a conversation is easy for most of us. But it's more difficult for computers because lots of things can sound like speech to them. To a computer, any sound—a cough, music playing, a slamming door, a crying baby—could be someone trying to communicate with it. It's only after analyzing the sound that the computer can determine whether or not it was speech.

In general, speech recognizers also need to know when a person has finished talking. It would be unfortunate if a caller started to say, "I'm leaving from Boston and going to San Francisco," but the computer cut her off after the first half of the sentence, then asked, "OK, and where are you going?" Conversely, it would also be frustrating for there to be an exceptionally long pause before the computer said something in response.

For all of these reasons, it's important for designers to understand the limitations and strengths of their speech recognizer—and to design the system accordingly.

WHY DESIGNING A SPEECH-RECOGNITION APPLICATION IS CHALLENGING

Think back to the AirTran example in Chapter 1. It was very short, wasn't it? Look how many points of discussion it raised—and we're only scratching the surface. Speech-recognition applications are powerful because they are *apparently* simple. Touchtone systems really are simple because callers know that their responses are limited to pressing any of 12 keys. And in a person-to-person conversation, people can reasonably expect that the person on the other end of the line can understand most spoken ideas. Speech-recognition systems fit somewhere in the middle. They have a seemingly natural interface, but the recognition application doesn't yet converse on a human level.

Callers don't know what the system can and can't understand if the system doesn't let them know the *parameters* (or degrees of freedom) of the interaction. Until the system tells them, callers don't know if they can ask *natural* questions, such as "What's the traffic like on I-93 South?" or if they must *first* indicate they want "Traffic information" and *then* indicate the route. It's up to the system (via the designer) to inform them.

Even the simplest questions can cause problems in a poorly designed speech-recognition system. For example, a large telephone company in the southern United States deployed a system back in 1997. Whenever this system attempted to confirm a caller's selection, it would ask, "Is that correct?" It was discovered that the system failed repeatedly when it came to that point in the conversation. Its designers were mystified. How could anyone misunderstand a question so simple and unambiguous? They assumed most callers would reply "Yes," "No," "Correct," "Incorrect," or some variation thereof. But even with all of these synonyms and variations programmed into the recognizer, there was still a high failure rate.

After listening to calls, the designers finally figured out the problem. Being gracious and polite southern folks, many of the callers were replying "Yes, ma'am" or "No, ma'am." The designers hadn't programmed that "ma'am" into the recognizer. A change was made to the system so that it recognized the phrases that callers said and within minutes of the change the problem was solved.

WHERE WE'VE BEEN—WHERE WE'RE GOING

The recognition technology is robust enough to enable the design of complex systems that have complex recognition tasks. This technology will constantly improve as the algorithms get better and computers get faster. And as we have seen, if the recognizer is tuned to understand the right words, the system can function correctly. But what constitutes the right words? In fact, what is underscoring the interaction between the caller and the recognizer? The right words are the words that the caller will know to say, be able to say easily, and may even utter when they haven't explicitly been asked. How can a designer know how to elicit these words from the caller? To better understand the elements and procedures of how to effectively design a speech-recognition system we have to understand the caller's psychology.

THREE

THE PSYCHOLOGY OF HOW PEOPLE INTERACT WITH SPEECH-RECOGNITION SYSTEMS

I rather think the cinema will die. Look at the energy being exerted to revive it—yesterday it was color, today three dimensions. I don't give it forty years more. Witness the decline of conversation.

—ORSON WELLES

Imagine two speech-recognition systems created for identical applications. Both have been carefully designed. Both have been rigorously tested for quality and usability. Both have been fine-tuned over the course of progressively broader deployment. But—for some reason—one system is more successful than the other. More callers use it—and they use it more frequently. What could possibly be the difference? To understand why some systems work better than others, it's essential to understand the psychology of how people interact with systems that *talk*—and the tremendous power of the voice.

Electronic devices that transmit or reproduce the human voice have been with us for over 125 years. The far-reaching impact of the first telephone was certainly not lost on Alexander Graham Bell, who had the first long-distance telephone system wired and operational within two years after he invented it in 1876. We who live in a world burgeoning with talking machines can barely imagine the visceral, emotional impact the early telephones and phonographs must have had on the general public. Within a few years, a world full of people who had never experienced anything other than face-to-face communications could hear the voice of a distant, beloved relative—or even the great Caruso himself!—in their own parlors. Nobody complained that the voices they heard on the phone were tinny approximations of the real thing or that Caruso's magnificent tenor sounded thinner and more brittle than a real *live* performance. Why not? Because the thing that mattered most—the emotional impact—came through loud and clear.

That also explains why, despite predictions by many to the contrary, television never made radio obsolete. By 1948 there were about one million televisions in homes throughout the United States, but millions of people were still listening to programs like *The Shadow* on the radio. Even today, despite the proliferation of cable TV channels and a vast wealth of video content, radio remains a vibrant and vital medium.

Of course, there's plenty of less-than-compelling audio and video programming out there. Talented directors, writers, and—yes, speech-recognition designers—can cause their audiences to feel a particular emotion, while others are less successful. What's the difference? Good directors, writers, and designers understand social psychology, even if it's something they have never formally studied.

One thing speech-recognition systems have in common with television, radio, and film is that they are mass media; they're designed for no one person in particular. *The Shadow* was created for an audience of millions—most of whom the writers and producers had never met. Think about your favorite movie. Had the director and actors of that film ever met you? Probably not, yet their work spoke to you. In an understandably less profound but no less engaging way, a good speech-recognition system makes an emotional connection with its callers.

This is all not just my opinion. It has been borne out in research studies that have explored the psychology of how people interact with media.

SOCIAL-PSYCHOLOGICAL RESEARCH

Among the most fascinating of the many experiments that have been conducted on the subject are the ones done by Stanford University professors Clifford Nass and Byron

Reeves and documented in their book, *The Media Equation: How People Treat Computers, Television, and New Media Like Real People and Places.* The following is a distillation of some of their findings.

The professors ran a series of studies to determine if the "rules" of social psychology (that had been tested thousands of times over the past century or so) would hold true not only for person-to-person interactions, but also for person-to-media interactions. They took some tried-and-true social psychological interactions (based on famous experiments dealing with flattery, reciprocity, expert opinion, and so on) and tested them using a person and a computer (or another media device, such as a television). Please note that these experiments did not deal directly with people interacting with speech-recognition systems, but rather people interacting with computers in a social way. Their results showed that people interact with media in the same way that they interact with other people and these media become **social actors** (that is, entities that emulate aspects of human behavior). Testing later conducted by the professors on speech recognition bore out the conclusion that speech-recognition systems are yet another media with which people interact adhering to the rules of social-psychological interaction.

The Flattery Experiment

In one experiment, when a computer randomly flattered people using a program (displaying words on the screen, such as "good job"), the participants in the study still felt flattered by the computer—even when they knew it was only the result of a randomizing program.

What are we to make of this? That lots of flattery in a speech-recognition system is a good thing? Well, no. I think any person subjected to prolonged episodes of random flattery will eventually be less moved—or perhaps even increasingly irritated—by such unwarranted praise. But it would be a different story if we designed a system to do what we would expect real people to do, that is, to flatter someone when that person has endured some arduous task to completion or made a sound, well-informed decision.

For example, if a person took the time to help a speech-recognition system learn more about their preferences, then perhaps a bit of flattery would be in order. I would also consider adding some flattering remarks to a speech-recognition prompt if a caller agreed to allow the client's affiliates to send them marketing material.

But I wouldn't stop there. I would then go on to do what real people also do: explain why I'm flattering the caller, as in the following example.

SYSTEM: You did a great job of rating all those products! Would you mind if we released your name, e-mail address, and preferences to some carefully selected partners of ours so that they can send you advertising?

CALLER: *OK.*

SYSTEM: That's great—we appreciate your allowing us to send you marketing material. Partner advertising helps us keep our costs low and pass along the savings to you.

The Reciprocity Experiment

When someone helps another person (either by giving them information, something tangible, or assistance), the person who has received help will feel obliged to reciprocate the aid. The experiment that tested this principle proved that people would try harder at a task if a computer *only tells them* that it is trying harder as well—even if the computer doesn't change its behavior at all.

Now, just for the record, I don't believe people—or even computers—should make a habit of lying, but as Machiavelli once pointed out, the end does occasionally justify the means. It's particularly useful when a system needs to motivate users to try harder at a task.

For example, in the Wildfire Communications, Inc. speech-recognition system, Wildfire, callers can teach the computer how to recognize their names when they call the system. If the system experiences difficulty recognizing a caller, it will ask that caller to use another method of identification (for example, saying or entering a phone number). At this point, the system attempts to learn once again how the caller pronounces his name, so that the caller won't need to enter his telephone number again in the future.

WILDFIRE: Sorry, I didn't recognize you. Would you like to take a moment to teach me how you say your name? Yes or no?

CALLER: *Yes*

WILDFIRE: OK, please say your name ....

The system goes on to collect the name a couple of times before saying, "Thanks, that will help for the next time you call."

Now, in reality, Wildfire does actually modify the way it recognizes the caller. However, when people call in and attempt to identify themselves the system may still not successfully recognize them. But, as this example shows, callers may be motivated to try a task again if the system asks them and promises to reward them in the future (in this case, by not requiring the caller to say or enter a phone number). The promise of future benefits establishes reciprocity—"scratch my back and I'll scratch yours"—and that invites cooperation.

ASK "DR." BLADE

I get a lot of questions about the psychological aspects of speech-recognition systems. Here are some of the more common questions—and my answers.

Should we use a male or a female voice for our system?

Social psychologists have found that in North America there are stereotypes associated with male and female voices. Male voices are seen as having more authority on technical matters, and female voices are seen as being more nurturing.[1]

If a speech-recognition system were to inform callers about something sensitive or depressing, perhaps a female voice would be more appropriate. Likewise, if we wanted a system to tell people how to fix their computers, they might prefer to hear it from a male voice.

There are other factors, however, a designer should consider when choosing the gender of a client's speech-recognition system. For example, what about the current spokesperson for the company—is it a woman or a man? What about the user population? Is it primarily male or female?

If we were to design a horse-betting application that needed to understand callers saying "Race three, three dollar trifecta, one-two-seven, over eleven-eight-three,

---

1. Clifford Nass and Byron Reeves, *The Media Equation: How People Treat Computers, Television, and New Media Like Real People and Places* (New York: Cambridge University Press, 1996), Chapters 14 and 15.

over nine," we might be tempted to choose a male voice, since the information is fairly technical. But I would disagree. I'm told that most people who bet on horse races are older men in their 50s, 60s, and 70s. I'd be inclined to think that these people would rather hear a smart, efficient, yet sexy female voice. So perhaps it doesn't always make sense to follow stereotypes. There are no hard-and-fast rules in choosing the gender of a voice for a particular company, but it is important to consider the psychological issues and not just the marketing ones.

Should we anthropomorphize our system?

People often ask me if a system should say things like "I'd like to do that, but ...." or "I'm sorry, I didn't understand you" rather than the more impersonal "We're sorry but ...." or "The system didn't understand you."

In all the work I've done for United Airlines, FedEx, and myriad other companies reaching millions and millions of people, the anthropomorphized, first person approach works best.

Speech-recognition systems should talk to people just as other people would talk to them, because ultimately the system is just another social actor, just like anyone else on the other end of the phone. These systems are unlike touchtone systems, which don't have the same necessity to say "I" because they don't really *listen* to callers in the same way that a speech-recognition system does. Also, it would sound strange for a system to refer to itself in the third person when it apologizes or provides information: "The system will read the following...." Huh? Which system? Some other system? I mean, unless we're talking about a speech-recognition system for Buckingham Palace, using the "royal we" only conveys a feeling of removed formality. This would undermine what speech-recognition systems do best—which is to work together, collaboratively, with callers to achieve a goal. Have you ever tried to set up a tent with someone who said "we" when they meant "I"? (Quite annoying: "We don't think that you're placing the pole correctly.")

In my experience, callers prefer anthropomorphized systems. For example, after a usability test for a flight information system, one usability test participant commented, "I felt that he (if I may call him that) really wanted to help me get the [flight] information I wanted."

Can a designer go too far with anthropomorphism?

Problems arise when a system acts as if it has feelings, is untruthful simply to manipulate people, acts overly familiar and chatty, preventing callers from completing their tasks in a timely manner. A good speech-recognition system is a lot like P. G. Wodehouse's Jeeves the valet—efficient, helpful, discreet, and unobtrusive.

Should speech-recognition systems be humorous?

Humor is fine, in the right context, and done in the right way. In fact, it's a great way to engage and disarm callers if they expect a stern-sounding, formal company. But it has its limitations—for a variety of reasons.

As every great comedian knows, in comedy, timing is everything. A speech-recognition system cannot be expected to know when a caller wants to hear a joke. And people sometimes see humor in a commercial setting as an indication that the company doesn't take its business or its customers' needs seriously.

To add a more universal form of humor, some systems use the aural equivalent of a sight gag. Wildfire had a *humor setting* that can be set from "low" to "high." In the high position, when a caller checking messages instructs the system to "Sort [the messages] the other way," Wildfire responds with the sound of cards shuffling before proceeding to the next prompt. It doesn't take much time, and it's evoked so rarely that most callers don't get tired of it quickly.

Also, most applications—particularly corporate call centers that handle tasks such as flight information, product orders, or rental car reservations—don't lend themselves well to humor. Actually, Southwest Airlines Co. is one airline that allows flight attendants to use humor when they recite the in-flight information. But consider this: if people call in to the same system often, that one joke is quickly going to become very tiresome—particularly since callers tend to pay more attention to a system on a phone then travelers do to flight attendants. Another reason to minimize humor is that it is highly subjective. The more diverse the calling population, the less likely it is that all of them will find a particular remark funny. If, on the other hand, the calling population is more homogeneous, targeted humor will be more successful.

What about those words like "Oops," "Oh!" and "OK?" You don't need those, right?

When people read my design documents they usually look at these small words and wonder, "Why are all these little words in here? We never use those in our touchtone system." And perhaps a system doesn't need to say particular words, like "OK" in the context of providing information, but it's a fast, easy, friendly way to let callers know that the system understood what they said before going on to ask the next question.

It's also polite and natural. Imagine a state motor vehicle department where the employees ask several questions in rapid-fire order without acknowledging they heard the answers.

CLERK: **Make of car?**
DRIVER: *Uh, Mercedes.*
CLERK: **Model year?**
DRIVER: *It's a 1970.*
CLERK: **Color?**
DRIVER: *Silver—well, silver-gray.*
CLERK: **Gray?**
DRIVER: *Well, I guess....*

People who are perceived as being polite and actively listening to someone never talk that way. They use linguistic discourse markers,[2] such as "OK" and "I see" to allow other people to better understand that their ideas are being understood. If the motor vehicle department employee were acting more like a human and less like a machine, the conversation would feel more polite, friendly and natural.

CLERK: **What's the make of your car?**
DRIVER: *Uh, Mercedes.*
CLERK: **OK. And the model year?**
DRIVER: *It's a 1970.*
CLERK: **Got it. What's the color?**
DRIVER: *Silver—well, silver-gray.*
CLERK: **All right, looks like we're done.**

---

2. Deborah Schiffrin, *Discourse Markers* (Cambridge, England: Cambridge University Press, 1987).

Words like "Oh!" can be used to reorient someone's thoughts. After a long instructional statement, a designer can add the word "Oh!" to shift the caller's attention to the last statement.

> SYSTEM: . . . and those are the primary commands you'll be using with this system. Oh! And if you ever get stuck, just say "Help" and I'll take things from there.

That one little word recaptures the caller's attention and highlights an important piece of information.

WHERE WE'VE BEEN—WHERE WE'RE GOING

It's helpful for us to gain an understanding of the principles and the psychological bases for designing particular elements of an application. The psychology of human–machine interaction permeates every aspect of the process of researching, designing, and evaluating a system. Let's examine this process in depth.

PART II

THE PROCESS OF DESIGNING SPEECH-RECOGNITION SYSTEMS

In Part I we explored the business case for automating data access and transactions over the telephone. And we covered the functional advantages of speech-recognition over touchtone technology. I also introduced some high-level design issues that concern us when we make a speech-recognition application.

As you'll see, there's a whole lot more to the process than simply figuring out which number on the keypad to assign to a given response. A speech-recognition system requires research—to learn as much as possible about the client's business and its customers. It requires a comprehensive, coherent design that incorporates every facet of the insights gained through the research, as well as an understanding of the psychology of how people interact with computers. Designs are embodied in Design Specifications, in which the most significant aspect are the prompts that must be written effectively if they are to create a successful application. The design and development must capture the client's branding requirements. The application requires rigorous usability testing—both before and after deployment—to ensure that it has been properly designed and implemented so that real callers can (and will want to) use it. Underlying all of these issues is the design philosophy. We can't achieve any of the other aspects of good design without a strong philosophical basis. We'll discuss these aspects from the designer's perspective in the chapters to come—as it's often the designer who assumes the responsibilities for these many roles.

FOUR

RESEARCH

To observe a fish, you must become one.

—JACQUES-YVES COUSTEAU

Be the ball.

—GOLFER TY WEBB (CHEVY CHASE) GIVING A PUTTING LESSON IN THE FILM *CADDYSHACK*

You begin the process of designing a speech-recognition system by developing a clear understanding of two things.

* What does the client/service-provider want to achieve?

* What does the caller want to do?

Designers need to perform meticulous research, because it is only through the detailed understanding of the system objectives that a designer can create and produce a successful application. To produce great speech-recognition systems, the designer needs to be many things, including

* A strategic thinker

* A master of logic

* A process expert

* A student of human nature

* A writer with a dramatist's ear for the subtleties of language and expression

Sometimes even a clairvoyant. (That's because the functionality is only one element of a speech-recognition system.) A well-designed speech-recognition system accounts for all aspects of the clients' objectives and their callers' objectives and needs.

CLIENTS' OBJECTIVES

Service providers don't introduce costly new technology to their customers unless there will be significant benefit to both the provider of the service as well as the user of the service. A clear set of objectives ensures that the designer understands the goals that must be achieved. These goals include

The business problem:	**What is the underlying issue that the system should solve? (E.g., enable around-the-clock self-service to customers who have traditionally not had that option.)**
The business objectives:	**What measurable results should the system accomplish? (Reduce costs? Improve customer satisfaction? Increase revenue?)**
The service:	**What service should the system provide to callers? (E.g., allow the callers to perform all their basic banking needs.)**
The application:	**What function—or functions—should the system perform? (E.g., a home banking system would allow callers to check balances, transfer funds, and perhaps reorder checks.)**

The business process/environment: How else do callers interact with the client?
How should these other channels influence the
design? (Does the caller have ATM access? And
if so, should the same language of the ATMs be
used in the speech-recognition system as well?)

It is essential to understand the business problem first, for several reasons. In some cases, the application a client wants may not be the best solution to the business problem. Understanding the business problem also provides you with essential clues to identify the system requirements, and enables both the client and you to measure and assess the success of the completed system. Some examples include reducing call center staffing costs by X%, or increasing annual revenue by $$Y$. Again, the idea is to provide measurable criteria for system performance.

In developing an understanding of the business needs, you must also be mindful of the other applications and channels that represent the client to the prospective callers. For example, in addition to branch offices, a bank might have a brokerage division with its own Web site and call center. You need to know how the speech application(s) will fit into this business model. Will the speech-recognition system be the primary point of contact between all callers and the client? Does the client want to encourage callers to use its corporate Web site or extranet?

In addition to answering these business objectives, you should also research the brand of the client company—its identity, positioning, messaging, and even its culture. The completed system needs to reflect and personify the company so that callers believe that the system is an extension of the company. If the sound of the speech application *doesn't* reflect the brand or tone of the company, callers might find their experience cognitively dissonant and confusing. After all, you wouldn't expect Ben & Jerry's Ice Cream to sound or act like John Hancock Financial Services, right?

Researching the character of a client company provides a deeper understanding of how the speech-recognition system should speak and behave to callers. This research helps you form an impression of how the completed system should sound. Ideas about vocal quality, tone, type, and use of language will eventually translate into the final design through both textual channels as well as in the production of the audio.

CALLERS' OBJECTIVES AND NEEDS

Users of these systems also have goals—but those goals are usually different than those of the service provider. To design a system that is well received by the intended audience, it's necessary to understand the following.

The application need: Why will callers call? (E.g., because they don't have the ability to go to a branch of their bank in which to perform basic banking tasks during normal business hours, thus requiring off-hour service.)

The application objective: What will callers hope to accomplish with the system? (A basic banking application should allow a vast majority of callers the ability to perform all the tasks that they associate with basic banking, and perhaps more. However, systems that don't satisfy callers' objectives won't be well received and may be underutilized.)

The caller's profile: What are the demographic attributes of the callers? What is their skill/education level, background, familiarity with technology, and so on?

The caller's frame of mind: Will callers be angry? (If they can't get the information they want easily.) Anxious? (Because they lost their credit card.) Excited? (Because they're booking a vacation.)

The most fundamental question to ask ourselves about callers is: Who are they? Often callers are the clients' current customers, employees, and business partners. But not always. Sometimes a company wants to appeal to a new group of people—or the application is so new that there is no existing caller base. What difference does it make who the callers are? A lot—because we all speak in different ways to different people. How we speak to friends is different from how we speak to strangers. And when we're trying to sell something rather than provide service to an irate customer—again, we speak differently.

What do you need to know about the callers to design a system? A good starting point is basic demographic data—age, gender, education, income level, and so on. This information will tell you whether the caller population is homogeneous or heterogeneous, and help you sharpen your focus on particular elements of research. If there were, for example, a system that served two different types of callers, hurried business people and the elderly, perhaps the system would have to try to accommodate these different users. If the caller population includes two or more groups with divergent needs—for example, business partners and direct customers—you need to create a system that quickly identifies each caller and sends them down appropriate paths.

Knowing who the callers are—and their relationship to the client—is the first essential step for us to understanding them. The best system designers take the time and effort to really get inside the heads of prospective callers. What do callers expect from the call? What do they want to accomplish? What is their mental state? Are they looking for fast answers or more personalized interaction? Will they need calming reassurance or "just the facts?"

How callers think about their tasks can make a big difference. For example, a bank that prohibits callers from talking to an agent before entering their 15-digit account number may receive many complaints from people who have lost their cards and urgently need a replacement. These callers are typically upset, want quick service, and won't have their account number memorized—thus preventing them from getting an expedient resolution to their problem. This system fails to help them efficiently resolve their problem.

But how do we get this more detailed information about caller needs and attitudes? One obvious way is to ask the service provider. But it shouldn't end there. Human nature being what it is, service providers aren't always the most reliable source of information about their callers and their feelings. A credit card provider may not have ever considered the mental state of callers who have lost their credit cards and how that relates to the design of a system. The touchtone system of the credit card division of MBNA America Bank[1] requires the caller to listen to prompts for approximately 45 seconds and asks for the credit card number. (Note that if the caller presses "zero" too soon, the system says "Sorry, that account number wasn't recognized," and then starts to play some options.) Eventually a list of five options is played, where the fourth one is for a "lost or stolen credit card." This process can take well over a minute—an eternity to a frustrated and concerned caller. And while callers might understand that the very first option of the system may not be "Press 1 for a lost card ... otherwise, please enter your credit card number," they will be a little frustrated by the time the system very calmly, and with a few too many words, tells them that the next available representative will help them. Even on their Web site, the home page and the 622-word site map have no reference to lost or stolen credit cards.

---

1. Based on the system design as of August 31, 2002.

Perhaps their card members don't lose many cards, and if they do they're very calm about it. But if we were to examine how people react when they lose a credit card, we'd imagine that they're not calm, nor are they willing to do much more then press the zero key on a phone repeatedly, or do a very cursory search on a Web site. If we contrast this design to the Web site offered by MasterCard Cardholder Solutions, Inc. (http://www.mastercard.com), we'll find that on the home page, the first option in a list of eight is for "Emergency Services"— clicking on that provides comprehensive text with a large-type phone number (1-800-MC-ASSIST).[2] Do both of these companies satisfy their users? And how does a designer know what to do when there are competing ideas about how to treat the caller?

A very good way, of course, is for us to go straight to the callers themselves.

As designers, we must directly observe how callers currently interact with the service provider. Obtain touchtone and Web data when possible. Visit call centers and listen to *live* calls. Interact with callers directly via focus groups or questionnaires. There's no such thing as too much user data (unless the process of digesting it slows down the designer too much). It's all worthwhile—and it all enhances our ability to *be the caller* and build a better system.

ASPECTS OF RESEARCH

Performing research for a speech-recognition system is not done in a vacuum; there is always a goal on which to focus as we gain more information. Elements of this include researching with an eye toward creating an *easy-to-use application*, where the *terminology* is audience-appropriate. A helpful technique is to perform a *morphological analysis* to examine the problem at hand by looking at other similar problems and relating informa-tion gleaned from those solutions to our own. Particularly in a speech environment, it's important to look at these situations carefully and understand that there can be a differ-ence between *what clients say they want and what they actually want,* the speech system to do—they may be two different things. We also must examine limitations that may limit aspects of the system by performing *feasibility* and *risk assessments.*

---

2. Based on the Web site as of September 1, 2002.

It's important to remember that when you finish the research phase, you should have a full understanding of the requirements of the system. At that moment the designer and the client will agree on what the completed system will comprise. This will all be documented in a **Requirements Specification.**

Usability

The most successful products are usually those that are designed for the needs of a specific audience. Apple Computer's original Macintosh computer is a great example. Because the Mac was intended to be "a computer for the rest of us," its developers made it as simple to learn and use as possible. To ensure that you create a system that works for its intended audience, you also need to research the callers' level of knowledge and sophistication and how they will use the product. Designers who intimately understand the people who will use their product create the most usable systems.

Jargon/Terminology

One of the most vital aspects of designing a speech-recognition system is to learn how people talk about their tasks. For example, did you know that flight attendants almost never "book" flights when they want to travel? Instead, they "list" a flight. To them, *booking* means paying for a flight—and free airfare is one of the great perks of working for an airline. So, it wouldn't be appropriate to design an application serving flight attendants that asks, "Would you like to book that flight?" Many of them might hang up, thinking they would have to pay for tickets. If designers of such a system had only read an overly simplified Requirements Specification (perhaps presented to the designer by the client) outlining the functionality of the system—but had not researched the calling population themselves—they probably wouldn't have designed the right question (or prompt).

Morphological Analysis

One of the most common ways designers solve problems is by drawing parallels to previous problems or real-life experiences. This approach can be particularly useful when designing a speech-recognition system due to the relatively few deployments of speech systems (in comparison to graphical user interfaces). By performing **morphological analyses**, the designer compares similar design solutions and how they relate to one another, and can analyze that design space in a structured way.

To perform a morphological analysis literally means to analyze the structure of something, but here the definition is expanded to include the analysis of features as well. For example, if we were asked to design a new VCR, we might look at many of the popular (and not so popular) VCRs and other similar types of video playback/recording systems (like TiVo and DVD players) sold today, and compare them to each other. We would create a grid, listing all the devices on one axis and their features on the other. By placing marks in the grid to specify which models have which features, we could begin to see trends forming. For example, we would learn that all video delivery methods have a *play* function, but very few of them have one-touch recording of live TV. Table 4.1 illustrates what the beginning of a morphological chart for VCRs and other video delivery systems might look like.

Different designers may very well draw different ideas from these data. For example, one designer might conclude that because the one-touch recording feature is rare, having this feature on a new VCR would help differentiate it in the marketplace and generate sales. Another designer may think that if the feature is so rare, it might not be something that consumers want. I assume that very few designers would think that a consumer VCR shouldn't have a play/pause feature, but perhaps someone could make a compelling case for it. The point is, each designer may draw a different set of conclusions from a common set of data—and design a different solution as a result.

TABLE 4.1 A Morphological Analysis of Video Playback/Recording Systems

Features	Video Delivery System				
	VCR Model 1	VCR Model 2	DVD Player 1	DVD Player 2	TiVo
Provide TV programming info	※				※
Play/pause action	※	※	※	※	※
Cable box control	※	※			※
One-touch recording of live TV		※			※

Sometimes it's helpful to expand the morphological analysis beyond the obvious comparisons. A person designing a VCR might learn something important—or become inspired—by performing a morphological analysis of audio cassette players or other related devices. For example, some cassette players have built-in headphone jacks with a separate volume control. Perhaps a designer would choose to market a VCR with its own headphone jack, so that people could connect the VCR directly to their headphones instead of their TV (which often don't have headphone jacks) or instead of running the sound through an amplifier. This could be an attractive feature for people who want to watch videos without disturbing others. We might not think of potentially worthwhile design features for speech-recognition systems if we don't look to other systems and solutions for inspiration.

But how can we perform morphological analyses with speech systems? At the moment, there aren't as many types of speech-recognition systems in the world as there are VCRs, so it's not easy to compare them directly to each other. However, we *are* able to compare the various features of different types of systems that perform similar tasks.

If we wanted to design a telephone-based banking system using speech recognition, we could examine the features of different banking channels (phone, Web, live-teller, ATM, and so on). By comparing these different channels, we could gain an understanding about the kinds of features to put in a speech system. Table 4.2 shows how the beginning of a banking morphological chart might look.

This simple analysis might suggest that the speech-recognition system should perform all the tasks that the touchtone system can, as well as some others that can be automated

TABLE 4.2 A Morphological Analysis of Banking Features

Features	Banking Channels			
	Branch	ATM	Web	Touchtone
Talk to agent	※			※
Withdraw funds	※	※		
Get account balances	※	※	※	※
Find a check	※		※	※
Reorder checks	※		※	

using a speech-recognition system. In this hypothetical example, we might know that a large number of people reorder checks most often because they move, rather than because they just want the next checks in their series. We might also discover that the reason the touchtone system doesn't have this feature is due to the complexity of collecting an address using only touchtone input. From this we could conclude that the speech-recognition system should have this feature, aiding in offloading this task from the bank representatives.

Every speech-recognition system is a service channel—and it can provide many types of services. That's why it's important to know not only what services the system will provide, but also what services it *will not* provide. Besides helping to determine the scope and structure of the system, understanding the limitations of the system can allow you to create a system that prevents caller confusion or frustration. For example, if a system provided a variety of information, such as weather, stocks, horoscopes, and breaking news stories, a caller might reasonably assume that the system would also provide related news-like information, such as traffic reports. If, however, this system does not include that functionality, the design needs to make sure that the caller doesn't expect to find that information there, or accommodates callers by allowing them to ask for that information and then letting them know that the system doesn't perform that function. When you understand the scope of the services to be provided, you can make sure the prompts and menu options are clear, specific, and help callers form an accurate mental-model of the system.

What Clients Say versus What Clients Want

It is the rare client or caller who will tell the designer exactly what he or she wants in a speech-recognition system; most clients simply don't understand the technology and design issues well enough to know its capabilities and limitations—particularly since technologies and standards change over the course of months and years. However, sometimes people will say they require a particular feature that may not be feasible or even possible for the designer to provide. In these cases, the designer must try to extract the underlying need behind the request for that feature and consider the ramifications of excluding it or think about ways to design around it.

For example, if we were trying to design a flight information system, and we asked several people what they wanted to know about their flights, many of them might tell us that they want to know "when the plane is going to arrive." If we were to interpret this requirement literally, we might have the design provide the exact time of arrival—"Flight 1687 will arrive at 6:02 P.M." If, however, those people actually want to know if the flight is on time or delayed, then you might adopt a broader interpretation and change the prompt to say "Flight 1687 is arriving *on time*, at 6:02 P.M." This prompt goes one step further by telling the caller that everything about the flight is going according to plan. In the first prompt—"Flight 1687 will arrive at 6:02 P.M."—the system simply reports the information but doesn't tell the user the most important information—the status of the flight.

Another way to examine this is to think about the delayed flight. Let's say we were about to take a trip and we called the airline to check on our flight, which was scheduled to depart at 1:55 P.M. If the system response only said "Flight 16 is leaving at 4:45 P.M."— a three-hour difference from our expectations—we might think we had received information about the wrong flight. But if the system replied, "Flight 16 is delayed and will be leaving at 4:45 P.M.," we would gain important additional information to clarify the situation.

An airline might also want to include the on-time information if its high on-time record is one of its key marketing messages and competitive differentiators. Good designers account for the functional considerations of an application as well as the marketing considerations.

As these examples illustrate, it's not enough to ask clients what information they want the system to provide; you must also understand their intention.

Feasibility Research

Although technology is advancing rapidly, all speech-recognition systems have limitations. These may be technical (the capabilities of the speech-recognition engine are limited), time-related (the design schedule may be extremely tight), resource-related (the client database experts are too busy), or language-related (the application is multilingual and simple translation won't ensure a usable system). Before designing the application, the designer needs to understand those inevitable limitations—and their implications.

But understanding the limitations is only one aspect of a larger issue—feasibility. A particular design feature may be desirable to the client or callers, but it may not be feasible because of cost, complexity, resource issues, schedule deadlines, or performance requirements. In such cases, you must work with the client to develop a more feasible alternative, or determine whether the feature is essential to the success of the application.

Designers must know the limitations (particularly the technical ones) so they can design something that will actually work. That sounds obvious—and it is—but it is extremely important, because as designers start the brainstorming process, they will be better prepared to let their ideas flow if they know the boundaries. And of course, boundaries are not always absolute or even detrimental; some of the best ideas come when designers are confronted with barriers to overcome or work around.

Risk Assessment/Hazard Analysis

Many designs don't pose any risk to callers or clients, but if, for example, a system could mistakenly execute a stock purchase or sale (or worse, options trade!), or if a system could reveal sensitive corporate or personal data, then appropriate security measures must be taken to ensure that certain errors do not occur. There are several ways to secure a system, but during the research phase designers must first determine what risks the system could pose to callers or clients so that these issues can be dealt with in the design.

A simple way to evaluate risk is to determine if a user error is **recoverable** or **unrecoverable**. A recoverable error is one that can be easily rectified. For example, if a system were to transfer funds incorrectly from one linked bank account to another (perhaps due to a recognition error), then the caller could simply move the funds back and rectify the situation. However, imagine what would happen if a system were to buy the wrong stock; the caller might not be able to recover from the error before the price of the stock dropped. This unrecoverable error could lead to lawsuits and potential financial ruin (for either the company or the caller!).

By asking clients "What's the worst that could happen?"—*before* the system is designed—you can build in security features that are needed to prevent or minimize the risk of such a worst-case scenario from ever occurring. Some typical security features range from design practices to technologies. For example, after a caller logs in to a stock trading system using an account number and a PIN number, we might assume that the caller is in control for the rest of the call and there is no further need to verify their identity. However, many callers and service providers want to ensure that neither the system nor the caller accidentally executes the wrong trade either due to errors with the speech recognition technology or due to a willful intruder who has taken control of the call.

Several steps can be taken to protect both parties. First, the system can explicitly confirm a trade and not allow a caller to interrupt the prompt while it's playing. Second, the caller can then either be required to enter or say his PIN number again, or enter or say a separate trading pass code to confirm the trade. Sometimes a caller might become familiar with the touchtone equivalents for some of the commands. Typically a system would assign the 1-key to indicate a confirmation, and the 2-key to indicate a negation (as in "Is that correct? Say 'Yes' or press 1 or 'No' or press 2"). However, it would be preferable to assign different keys, such as the 7-key as the confirmation key and the #-key as the negation in an attempt to prevent people from accidentally pressing the 1-key when they mean to press the 2-key, and vice versa.

And last, there is technology known as **voice authentication** or **speaker verification**, the best of which enables a system to simultaneously verify that the person is saying a particular pass phrase as well as verifying the biometrics of her voice print as previously registered. And of course, all these methods could be used together to ensure even more security, but that's not always necessary.

ASSEMBLING A REQUIREMENTS SPECIFICATION

Once you complete all the research, you'll be ready to write the Requirements Specification document. The Requirements Specification answers the question "What needs to be done to make the system real?"

not:

"*How* will the system work?"

The Requirements Specification is essentially an agreement between the designer and the client that:

1. **The designer does indeed understand the client's needs, the objectives of the systems, and for whom the system will be deployed.**

2. **The designer will perform what is spelled out—and no less.**

Most of the time, a client doesn't mind if a design does more than is described in the Requirements Specification, so long as it doesn't exceed the budget or cause schedule slippage.

The reason that you should not describe the specifics of *how* the design will work is because usually at this point you have not fully considered all aspects of the solution. Therefore, there is a risk of setting the client's expectations either too high or too low.

It's best to think of the Requirements Specification as part recipe (where all the particulars of the system are clearly spelled out) and part story (a description of how the system will feel). Keep in mind that the language of this document doesn't need to be stilted and stuffy. It should be written in simple, vivid language because often this document will be read by a variety of people, including lawyers, project managers, technical specialists, marketing managers, and vice presidents. You should ensure that it flows clearly from *big picture* ideas to specific details. Above all, the Requirements Specification needs to be cogent, because the contractual obligations between the designer and the client will be based on it.

Included in the document are:

1.   A description of the overall functional goal of the system.

Example: The system will allow callers to conduct banking transactions from any telephone.

2.   A description of the callers and calling behavior.

Example: 80% of the callers are expected to be in their 30s with an average income of $45,000 a year. They are expected to call in to the system from home about 50% of the time, from work 25% of the time, and from other locations, including the outdoors, 25% of the time.

3.   A description of the specific functions of the system.

Example: The caller will be able to transfer funds among savings, checking, and money-market accounts only. However, a caller might have up to three accounts of each type that may differ only in the account number.

4.   A description of the database functionality that will provide the information to the application and the components to be used.

Example: The database will provide the system with all the customer's account information based on their account number.

The Requirements Specification may state that the client will provide certain things that don't currently exist. For example, the client might have to change the database to work in a different way to support a particular functionality. By putting this in the document, the designer is assured that the system will work as planned once it's completed. A typical example of how the database might be expanded is when a speech system would be able to take advantage of knowledge of usage patterns of the caller. In this case the ability of the speech system to be able to store just a few bytes of data can allow the system to *remember* what actions the caller has or has not performed in the past and can teach the caller new functionality of the system—on a personalized, as-needed basis.

5.   A description of the *feel* of the system, including any elements of the company brand.

Example: The company's audio logo and tag line will be used when the system greets the caller.

The Requirements Specification should discuss the *feel* or stylistic elements of the system, such as the type of language used in the prompts (formal or informal) and any elements of the company brand that need to be incorporated. For example, if Intel created a speech-recognition system, they may want it to include the four-note audio logo used in their TV commercials. A bank may want to specify that the text of the prompts be consistent with the exacting, grammatically correct style of its literature.

6.   A list of specific, measurable goals for the system.

Example: The system will enable 90% of callers to complete 95% of their transactions.

This is a key component of the Requirements Specification, because it provides a yardstick for measuring and evaluating the success of the system. The goals can be both objective and subjective. Here are a few more examples.

* 70% of callers surveyed after using the system will give it a rating of seven or higher on a ten-point scale.

* 99% of callers will understand every word the system says.

* 80% of callers will never need to invoke "Help" after they've used a particular function of the system twice.

ANTICIPATING CHANGE

One final thought. Before beginning the design process, the designer needs to anticipate that change will occur—and that the speech-recognition system must be flexible enough to change along with it.

Future-proofing a system requires a certain degree of clairvoyance. The designer must think ahead to the client's future needs, and design the system to accommodate them with minimal reengineering. That means anticipating the use of new technology, introduction of new services, adaptation of the application to new languages, and redesign of customer-facing communications, such as Web sites, advertising tag lines, and corporate logos.

This holds true even if the system is only a temporary solution, because temporary solutions have a funny way of becoming permanent. In Cambridge, Massachusetts, for example, there is a subway station with a large parking lot located very close to the intersection of two major highways. To get people out of the parking lot and onto the two arteries, the engineers erected a temporary solution incorporating several traffic lights, roadways, and a merge lane. To work effectively, the merge lane requires drivers to merge every other car at very fast speeds—not unlike something you might see at a closely choreographed auto thrill show. It's always easy to spot the new drivers, because they're too timid to merge quickly and inevitably miss the entire light cycle. Even for experienced drivers, this intersection is nerve-wracking at rush hour. This *temporary solution*—which the supervising engineer deemed totally unacceptable—has remained in place for over 20 years.

There's another benefit to designing a system to accommodate future change. The more flexible a system design is, the more likely it is that the client will invest in future changes—and use the same designer to ensure that the ideas and paradigms in the current system are continued in the new one.

WHERE WE'VE BEEN—WHERE WE'RE GOING

Once the research phase has been completed, you will be ready to take what you've learned and start executing the design. There is not always a clear line between when research ends and design begins—they always seem to overlap. But now that we know more about what we need to learn before designing, let's move on to discussing the ideas unique to the design of speech-recognition systems.

FIVE

DEVELOPING THE DESIGN

The Sleeping Beauty **may well be the best of all my works, and yet I wrote it incredibly quickly.**
—PETER ILICH TCHAIKOVSKY, WHO COMPOSED THE BALLET SCORE IN LESS THAN THREE WEEKS

Art has to move you and design does not, unless it's a good design for a bus.
—DAVID HOCKNEY

At this point in the process the designer should have amassed a wealth of client and user research, and developed a thorough understanding of the company's brand. This is when the ideas should start to percolate—if they haven't already. In fact, by now many designers may already have a fairly clear idea about where they want to go with their designs. It's at this stage that the designer can, and must, go into full-tilt design mode—starting to correlate all the research they've gathered to develop the design.

What does a design for a speech-recognition system look like? Basically, it needs to convey the particular experience the designer intends to provide a particular caller. A design must first be expressed primarily through the written word, but sometimes with audio components as well.

Now, before we go any further, let me be clear about one thing. This chapter is *not* intended to teach you how to be a great speech interface designer—as that is a skill that takes time and practice. Rather, my goals here are

* To offer ideas on how to approach the process of speech interface design and how to *think* like a designer

* To provide a framework to help you focus your efforts and avoid wasted time and mistakes

* To share ideas about designing certain system components

If after reading this chapter you are intrigued enough to explore new design directions, then my work here is done. Because that's the only way any designer can improve his or her design ability—by doing more of it.

CONCEPTUALIZING AND BRAINSTORMING

The first step of the design process is to conceptualize. When I talk about conceptualizing, I'm not referring to an open-ended creative exercise removed from practicalities. Don't get me wrong—there are many opportunities to be creative in the design of a speech-recognition system. But that creativity must come in service to the real purpose of the design, which is to accomplish specific business goals and communicate specific messages. **Conceptualizing** is the process of translating those goals and messages into actual system content.

Sometimes the best way to begin to conceptualize a particular problem (or to get through designer's block) is to start brainstorming, either alone or with colleagues. This can be a fairly organized and productive activity, during which many ideas may be generated and recorded in a wide-ranging discussion. Brainstorming requires that a person (or persons) start generating ideas, even absurd ones—as long as they're related to solving the problem at hand. There's no limit to what can—or should—be considered during the brainstorming process. The goal is to collect as many good ideas as possible about as many aspects of the system as possible. No criticism of the ideas is allowed until after the initial brainstorming is completed. After this stage it's time to winnow down the ideas, categorize them, and rank them. A number of books on the market are available to help learn various techniques of brainstorming and how to facilitate good brainstorming sessions.[1]

Good ideas can come from anywhere, and brainstorming is a great way to find them. Of course, brainstorming can also generate a lot of really bad ideas—ideas that won't work because they're impractical, they haven't been well thought out, or they simply have the wrong style or feel. But don't automatically assume that these supposedly bad ideas are a complete waste of time. At worst, they can convince you what *not* to do, thereby leading to other, more productive directions. At best, they can act as springboards to really great ideas.

What kinds of ideas should be considered? Things like:

* How the call should flow from one state (or turn of the dialogue) to another

* How components of the system should handle certain tasks

* How the prompts should be worded

* How and where branding elements should be integrated (branding is discussed in detail in Chapter 7)

The answers aren't always obvious or simple. For example, should a banking system prompt the caller for the amount of a cash transfer *before* asking which account to transfer to—or vice versa? Which approach would minimize confusion and mistakes? Sometimes these answers will come from the research performed, other times brainstorming can help designers think through these questions.

In most cases, the biggest challenge isn't coming up with good brainstorming ideas—it's organizing all those good ideas into concepts.

---

1. Suggested reading for brainstorming: Michael Michalko, *Thinkpak: A Brainstorming Card Deck* (Berkeley: Ten Speed Press, 1994).

For example, let's say a brainstorming session generates 100 good ideas for everything from call flow to prompts to the use of corporate theme music. The designer can then organize these ideas into groups so that the tradeoffs between similar concepts can be evaluated on the basis of quality, priority, appropriateness, and feasibility. Keep in mind that some ideas are more vague than others and need to be treated as such. Sometimes, however, the ideas might fit into particular categories such as:

* Navigation commands

* Specific task handling

* Wording choices

* Call flow structures

* Database issues

* Need for additional technology (such as text-to-speech engines)

After grouping the ideas and evaluating them, you start conceptualizing individual elements of how the system will function and sound, looking for opportunities to make a design that makes the experience easier, faster, and more productive for callers. Here are a few examples.

* A banking system that provides the addresses of local branches could use Caller ID to automatically provide callers with the branch addresses closest to the area covered by that telephone exchange, rather than explicitly asking the callers the area that they're interested in.

* A system could identify callers after they provide their account number, and use the profiles of callers to provide only relevant options to them. So, for example, a banking system wouldn't offer "Credit card balance" for a customer who didn't have a credit card with that bank.

* A system could provide relevant information based on the time of day or calendar. For example, an IRS system could offer callers refund information at tax

filing season. Or perhaps a voice portal could be set up to provide weather and traffic information during commuting hours.

CONGRUENCE OF STYLE

From the brainstorming and ideation a single concept will begin to form. The designer narrows the field of ideas, and eliminates bells and whistles if they don't all work as a cohesive unit. A solid concept ensures that the design ideas work well for the audience. This continuity will make sure that the application feels like a single, integrated concept, rather than several disparate ideas stuck together.

Building trust and loyalty requires congruence in both interaction style and language. If we were designing a large system where we thought one technique for navigating through a large list was appropriate in one context while a different technique was more appropriate in another, callers could become confused because they would expect that list navigation should have a standard behavior throughout the entire application.

A feeling of discontinuity can drive a wedge between companies and their customers. Let's say a designer decided to use very casual language for one part of a banking application—perhaps omitting transaction confirmation numbers to make the system feel smoother. If the designer then opted to use very formal instructions for another part of the application—say, using a stern tone in directing the caller to write down and save important information—it wouldn't feel right. It would be like having a casual conversation with a friend when, suddenly in mid-conversation, the friend started speaking in legal terms. Incidentally, it works the other way, too. Most people who are accustomed to having, say, their brokerage firms speech-recognition system address them in a strict, formal tone would not appreciate it if the *employees* suddenly became casual and chummy.

Imagine that you were a surfer who went into a surf shop every week for several years, knew the owner well, and always paid for your surfboards and gear at the time of purchase. Suppose you visited the shop one day to buy a 50¢ bar of wax, but discovered that you left your money at home. What if, instead of treating you as a valued customer, the owner became stern and flatly refused to give you the wax until you came back with the 50¢? You wouldn't like that the style and tone of the interaction had changed, and the same holds true for how speech-recognition system callers need to treat callers.

Consistency

Consistency, used correctly, ensures ease of use. The problem is, designs inevitably change when a new designer takes over or augments a design—or even when designs are created over a long period of time and a new designer inadvertently changes the way they handle certain things. Left unchecked, this can make a design seem "choppy" or disconnected.

Consistency can be embodied in many ways.

- A consistent use of language to refer to similar ideas, or to allow callers to say the same commands in multiple places to elicit the same responses from the system (that is, if callers can say "Help" in one context to receive additional information, it would be inconsistent to require them to say "More information" in a different context).

- A consistent feedback structure can be manifested in the method the system employs to give feedback to callers indicating when it didn't understand them, or when it didn't hear them—the same way each time.

- A consistent use of audio effects can indicate that an action has been completed or that a caller has reached a particular point in an application.

Natural Flow

A good design needs to flow elegantly from one moment to the next so that callers can retain their sense of context and understand where they are in the call.

Let's say a design required a series of short questions. We wouldn't want to write each question to sound like a brand-new thought; rather we want the questions to sound like the continuation of a conversation both textually and in intonation. The following examples illustrate how to do this.

Instead of asking:

> *"On what date are you picking up the car?"*

... and then asking:

> *"At what time are you picking up the car?"*

... it would be much more natural and within the context to ask:

> *"On what date are you picking up the car?"*

... and then ask:

> *"And at what time?"*

The second exchange would sound very conversational, and would seem (and be) faster than the first. Since the context of "picking up the car" has been set, there is no need to repeat that in the subsequent question since the question is also subsumed under the first context—that is, it asks for a further clarification of the moment that the person will pick up the car.

Instead of having the system say:

> ***"Please enter or say your account number"***—*where the word "your" might refer to the "account number the person has access to" (a common task for brokers to do for many of their clients)*

… and then follow with:

> ***"I'm accessing your information"***—*where the word "your" refers to the caller's information, rather than the information associated with the account number*

... it would be better to have the system reply:

> ***"I'm accessing the account information"***—*where by using the word "the" we get around a potentially incorrect statement.*

It's important to remember that novice callers aren't simply using the system; they're also inductively learning it at the same time. The more consistent lists of options are, the easier it is for callers to learn the system. The sequence of commands in a prompt should only be altered if there is a compelling reason to do so.

Instead of asking:

> *"Would you like to 'Book the flight,' 'Change the itinerary,' or 'Talk to a representative?'"*

… and then in other contexts, relocate the "Talk to a representative" command by asking:

> *"Would you like to 'Make another reservation,' 'Talk to a representative,' or 'Review your account information?'"*

… it would be better to make sure that similar types of commands (particularly ones that spare users from frustration, such as "Talk to a representative") always appear in the same place in a list of commands. This way, users can quickly identify where they are in the prompt.

Consistency and naturalness also make the designer's job easier. The same language can be cut and pasted from one place to another when it needs to be repeated.

DEFINING THE CALL FLOW

When the designer has a strong concept and a complete set of ideas with which to express it, the task of designing the call flow can begin. This starts with representing it graphically, then mapping it into a textual form. **Call flow** simply refers to the structure of the design. This call flow takes callers through a series of states during which they will either be asked to respond to a question, listen to some information, or both.

In most applications, the first state is typically called the **welcome state**, in which the caller is welcomed to the application. At this point, depending on the application, the caller may or may not need to be identified. A home banking application would require the caller's account number, for example, but a purely informational application, such as a voice portal, would not.

Using the home banking example, the application would then need to verify the caller's identity by asking for a password or social security number. This usually takes the caller to the equivalent of a **main menu**—the starting point from which the caller can move into several states to get account information, transfer funds, set preferences, and so on.

When designing the call flow, the objective is to define the structure of the application. This can be as simple as creating a typical flowchart diagram. However, because the call flow and the prompt text are closely linked, it's often helpful to include notes describing how certain complex situations will be handled. The actual writing of the prompt text will come later.

Figure 5.1 illustrates a rudimentary call flow diagram, designed to show only the big picture of how people will move through the various *states* in the application.

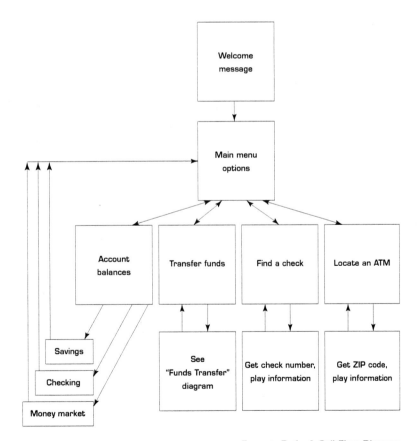

FIGURE 5.1 A Call Flow Diagram

Although the call flow diagram is a depiction of the structure of an application, it can also be used to convey design ideas and to help the designer think about various solutions. In my diagrams, I may not even draw all the arrows or include all the boxes if I need to describe a complex situation and I haven't quite worked out all the details. Instead, I might just draw some gray arrows and write a note to the reader describing the behavior that should logically follow, and flesh out the details later when I've gained more information or after I've had the opportunity to review the design.

A Real-World Example of a Call Flow

Let's explore the different ways to structure a call flow using a real example. I once designed a system for a large wholesale distributor that allowed its retail customers to call in and report two kinds of shipping errors. The client wanted the system to handle these errors and catalogue them appropriately.

This company shipped products to its retailers almost every day. Its speech-recognition application enabled retail staff (usually stock clerks) to report shipping errors and receive a credit toward their next shipment. The two types of shipping errors that could occur were

* A "shortage"—when an ordered item was missing from a shipment, or

* A "mis-pick"—when an incorrect item was substituted for an ordered item in a shipment

How might a designer create a call flow to handle this? The most common way that I've seen people design the solution looks like the one in Figure 5.2.

Although this approach would work, there are better ways to do it—if we first consider a few relevant factors. First, we need to understand the callers who would use the system. In this example, they were most often stock clerks—low-paid, entry-level workers with little interest or incentive to learn the manufacturer's jargon and processes. Instead, I opted for a way to handle the situation *without* requiring callers to answer questions like "Was there a shortage or a mis-pick?"

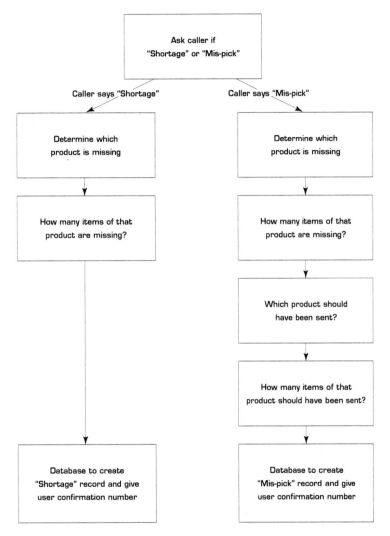

FIGURE 5.2 A Common Call Flow Solution

When we examine Figure 5.3, we can see overlaps and similarities in the structure.

Figure 5.4 shows how you can streamline the design and modify the approach by simplifying the questions for callers.

Often when I present this example, people ask me how it can handle the reporting of shortages and mis-picks to appropriate databases if they are collapsed from two states

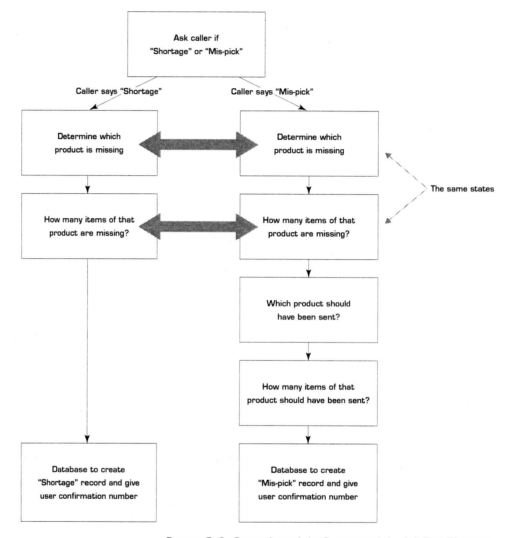

FIGURE 5.3 Comparison of the Structure of the Call Flow Diagrams

into one. This is an instance where a good programmer will decide how best to devise a reporting mechanism for this interface without compromising the design. The designer's objective and responsibility are to ensure the most elegant call flow, not to force the programmer to structure things in any particular way.

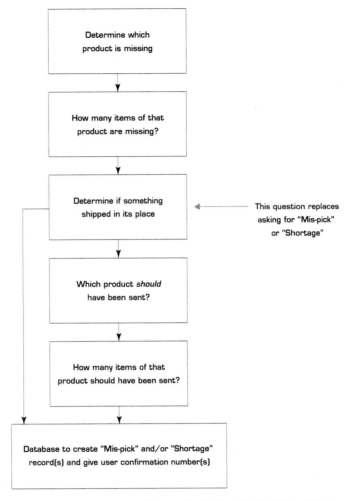

FIGURE **5.4** Simplified Call Flow Solution

In this example, the programmer could decide either to

* Build one state that handles all the complexities (but may involve more coding challenges), or

* Build several states (which may allow for easier coding and testing)

Either way, it's the programmer's decision—not the designer's.

The Top Five Tenets of Call Flow Diagram Design

1. Ensure that there's a one-to-one correspondence between the call flow and the diagram that represents the call flow (that is, each question or statement is represented in the call flow diagram).

2. Write a one-page, high-level overview of the entire application so that it's easy to see what functions the application will perform. This should be supplemented by as many detailed diagrams as necessary to describe the specifics.

3. Ensure diagrams are easy to read with descriptive words for each state.

4. Number all states in the diagram to facilitate searches within a word processing application, aid in visual searches when discussing the document with clients, and divide application functionality numerically (for example, all states beginning with the number four are regarding Funds Transfers, states beginning with the number five are regarding Account Balances, and so forth).

5. Organize and present the elements in the diagram for clarity, intelligibility, and easy navigation along the main path.

VISION CLIPS/SAMPLE CALLS

As an alternative—or an enhancement—to a call flow diagram, the designer may want to create a **vision clip** to describe how the application will work. This is a sample script that illustrates a *vision* of how the final version of the system might sound. (Not to be confused with a **sample call**, which typically refers to a recording of an actual exchange from a live system.) The clip is produced as an audio file, complete with sound effects or music. For many designers, a vision clip is a very easy place to start the creative process, because before they start drawing boxes and arrows on paper, they can quickly sketch out the sound—*and feel*—of the system and show and play it to other people for quick review.

Sharing a vision clip with a client is a great way for designers to initiate a discussion of their design ideas. But it's important to remind clients that the vision clip is only a rough draft and subject to change. A vision clip can also help jump-start the process of structuring the overall call flow.

All you need to do to create a vision clip is to form a grid like this...

Who's talking	What's spoken
SYSTEM:	
CALLER:	
SYSTEM:	
CALLER:	

... and then insert prompts in the places where the system speaks, and reasonable answers in the places where the caller responds. Although you may not have finalized what the system will ultimately do, the vision clip serves as an easy way for almost anyone to understand the design of the basic flow and feel of the system.

A simple vision clip for a banking system might look like this.

Who's talking	What's spoken
SYSTEM:	Welcome to the Big Bank of New England. Please enter or say your account number.
CALLER:	*Five, eight, nine, two, six, five, one, one, two, two, seven.*
SYSTEM:	<audio icon> Got it. What's your PIN number?
CALLER:	[Caller uses the touchtone keypad to enter a four-digit PIN]
SYSTEM:	Oh, hi! Welcome back. You're at the main menu. You can say "Account balances," "Transfer funds," "Find a check," or "Preferences."

Vision clips are particularly useful on large, multi-phase projects that begin with basic functionality and become more complex over time. By showing how the final version of the project will work, these vision clips can help clients understand how their initially sparse application will expand elegantly over time.

Uses of Vision Clips and Call Flow Diagrams

Designers should present vision clips to clients to launch a discussion on how the system will work—both *for* callers and *with* back-end databases. As clients read (or hear) the vision clips and then look at the diagrams, they gain a basic understanding of how the design handles the most common calls. The vision clips should, of course, be consistent with the Requirements Specification and will logically illustrate the salient elements of that document.

The Top Five Tenets of Vision Clip Design

1. Ensure that the vision clip captures one or more common scenarios callers will experience.

2. Produce vision clips that are highly illustrative of the salient functionality and not exhaustive of every possible case. Clients can generally extrapolate other similar or common cases from a well-chosen and produced vision clip.

3. Present secondary (and tertiary) clips to show off separate functions of the system, such as error handling, complex situations, or how the system works for different types of callers (that is, novices versus experienced).

4. Start by presenting the least complex vision clip when presenting several vision clips to a client. This vision clip should illustrate the designer's ability to craft a simple dialogue well. Then present the remaining clips in order of complexity, building on the fundamentals of the previous clips.

5. Use vision clips early in the design process since they enable designers to get early feedback from clients, and then rewrite them for another round of feedback before beginning the long process of creating the Design Specification.

THE DESIGN SPECIFICATION—CONVEYING THE DETAILS OF THE DESIGN

Once the vision clips have been made and the call flow has been finalized, the designer needs to flesh out and annotate the rest of the design details. These expressions of the design are collected in the **Design Specification**. The Design Specification needs to be clear, thorough, well thought out, and specific. This is the document programmers will use to implement the design.

There is no official format to follow in creating a Design Specification, but I recommend the following five sections that cover the following areas.

Goal of the Section	Potential Document Manifestation
To give an overview of the document	A short paragraph that describes who should read this document and the purpose of the document, particularly as it relates to other technical documents that will be produced as part of the total effort.
To summarize what the document contains and how it will express the design	This may include a list describing the sections of the document such as document change history, aesthetics, and a reduction of relevant caller profile information from the requirements specification, as well as notes about the conventions used to textually express the design.
To provide examples of how the final version of the design will work	This can be in the form of sample call scripts or descriptions.
To illustrate a detailed, visual representation of how the overall system will work functionally	This section can be a series of diagrams that range from an overview to a granular level illustrating the connections and paths that the caller may take through the application.
To show state (or turn of the dialogue) descriptions	A complete, comprehensive view of how the system will work in each state (each time the computer asks a question)—providing enough detail so that a developer could easily program from it and so that a nondeveloper can understand the essence of that state.

CONSTRUCTING A DESIGN SPECIFICATION

One way to create a detailed Design Specification is simply to make a table for each state that has been defined (that is, each box in the call flow diagram). By including the elements listed below (along with any other pertinent development-specific information) for any given state, the designer can make things much easier for the programmer.

* The name of the state (and its state number).

* The names of the state(s) that lead into it.

  For example, callers may enter the "main menu" state from the "welcome" state.

* The names (and/or unique numbers) of the prompts.

  The prompt types—for example, initial, retry, timeout, and help—refer to the various common prompts used in many speech-recognition systems (more on these prompt types and writing them will be found in Chapter 6.)

* The text of the prompts to be played to the caller and any conditional statements about when to play them.

  For example, a particular prompt might be played only to expert or repeat callers, while a more verbose prompt would be played only to novice callers at that point in the call. For example, novice users might hear, "Enter or say the phone number, being sure to include the area code"—compared to the expert user who hears, "What's the phone number?"

* Any spoken words or phrases the system will need to recognize, and the touchtones that will be recognized (as a backup to the speech recognition).

  A typical system would have a list of commands, such as "Transfer funds," "Find a check," and so on. Also listed would be synonyms for these commands as well as the set of recognized touchtone equivalents.

Command	Synonyms (if any)	Touchtone equivalent
Transfer funds	Transfer Funds transfer	1
Find a check	None	2
Account Balance	Balances Account information	3

* The *go to* statements for each recognition.

  For example, when the system recognizes a banking caller who says "Transfer funds" or presses the appropriate touchtone key, it should "go to" a state named "5100 transfer funds, first state, get amount."

* Any special prompts needed to confirm recognition of a caller.

* Special notes about the state.

  For example, "Don't let the caller interrupt the prompt when playing the confirmation message." These may also be notes to the programmers explaining how to handle special cases, like "Don't play the default apology prompt when the system makes a mistake. Instead, play prompt number 12005: "Oops, let's try again...."

Figure 5.5 shows what a typical state might look like (along with some call-out boxes, explaining the elements of the state).

This diagram illustrates a state called "2100_Finance_Forex_Menu," which a caller can only enter from states called "2000_Finance_Menu." The list of potential prompts that can be played to the caller is in the prompts type section (for example, initial prompts are played when a caller first enters the state, while a timeout prompt is played only if the system doesn't hear any information), the name of the prompt (in this case the names are numbers in which the first four digits are the same as the number of the state and the last digit is unique). Next to the name of the prompt, the actual words of the prompt are written, as in prompt 21001, "For which currency would you like to hear the exchange rate?"

Below the Prompts section is the section that describes what the recognizer is listening for, either the currency amount or a command. The currency amount is written in

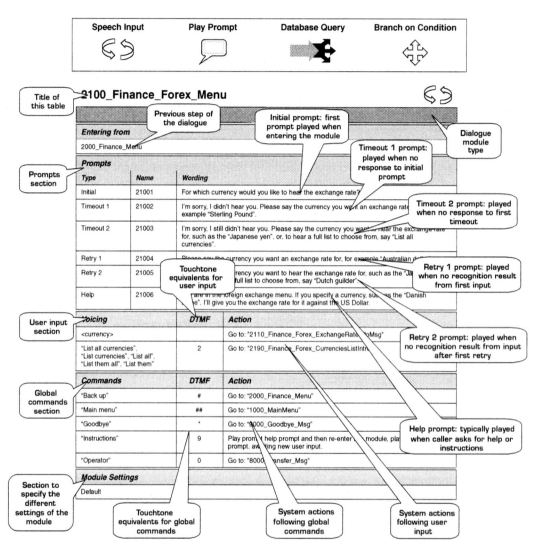

FIGURE 5.5 Sample State Table

brackets to indicate that a complete definition can be found in an appendix; this term would be too complex to define in this one section and may be used in several places in the application. In addition to the command, any synonyms for that command are included, as in "List all currencies" and "List them." The touchtone equivalents are written in corresponding cells that can be used in place of spoken commands. Next to those cells is the action that should be taken when the caller responds with an appropriate response. There is also a section for notes on the bottom (in this example it's called "Module Settings") that can be used to describe any other settings, such as those that are unique to the technology used.

FOLLOWING THROUGH ON THE INITIAL DESIGN PHASE

After the initial phases of the design process have been completed, the designer needs to follow through by asking two fundamental questions.

- *Does the design meet the original goals of the system?* All this takes is a review of the Requirements Specification to ensure that all goals relating to call flow and prompts have been met. (Any goals relating to brand and identity will be addressed later, during production.)

- *Are there situations in the design where the caller or the client could get into trouble?* For this, you can perform a simple hazard analysis by reviewing all the situations that could get a caller into trouble, and then modifying the design to eliminate or reduce the risk of such errors occurring. To do this analysis correctly, you need to determine what kinds of errors can occur in the call at any given point. For example, if a particular system in the U.S. needs to be compliant with the Americans with Disabilities Act (ADA) but does not have a touchtone fallback for every command, then the company may face legal action.

WHERE WE'VE BEEN—WHERE WE'RE GOING

We've begun to explore the underpinnings of the design process, two ways to express the design—both textually in a script used to illustrate a facet of the design and textually in the form of a Design Specification that articulates the intricate details of how the design will function. From the design perspective, the way that the system speaks is as important, if not more important, than how it listens. Examining how to craft the words the system says is the topic of our next chapter.

WRITING EFFECTIVE PROMPTS

A writer is somebody for whom writing is more difficult than it is for other people.

—THOMAS MANN

Writing is easy. All you do is stare at a blank sheet of paper until drops of blood form on your forehead.

—GENE FOWLER

The difference between an adequate speech-recognition system and a great speech-recognition system lies in how the system asks questions and conveys complex information. Great systems do it with an elegance worthy of a haiku; their meaning and impact are clear and immediate, and not a single word is wasted. The more elegant a system is, the more intuitively—and quickly—a caller can use it, and the greater value it offers to both clients and callers.

This chapter does not discuss topics such as "the *best* way to ask a 'yes/no' question." Why not? Because, for one thing, there *is* no single "best way." Rather, there are many different ways to properly ask a "yes/no" question, depending on the situation. I've avoided absolute rules—and words like "always," "never," "best," and "worst"—because the state of the art of design is constantly changing. Any absolute rules I could offer would soon be outdated. In fact, I prefer that people understand and extract the underlying ideas about the design of successful speech systems rather than blindly follow a set of rules.

THE LANGUAGE OF ASKING QUESTIONS

At its most basic level, the design of speech-recognition system prompts is composed of two elements:

* Questions the system asks

* Statements the system makes

The questions that are asked need to be clear and not easily misinterpreted, and the statements need to provide useful information, in a valuable format. And most of the time there is a mixture of statements to inform the caller, and questions by which the system will glean new information, in the same context. This can get tricky when the conversations between the computer and the caller start to get complex. Most people don't realize how much error correction they do in *real* conversations. How often do our conversations with real people sound anything like the carefully scripted conversations of a TV drama? On TV and in movies, characters never say "Uh, what? I didn't get that last thing you just said."

In real life, real people do lots of error checking and correcting. And when we're asked to clarify something we've said, what do we do? We usually rephrase it or provide further information. If the people to whom we're talking need further clarification, we might even explain why we're asking the question.

Speech-recognition systems need to emulate this behavior, because—just as in real conversations—mistakes and misunderstandings do occur. Think of all the things that could possibly go wrong when a system asks a caller a question.

* The caller may not respond.

* The caller may respond with the wrong answer and the recognizer can't understand the response.

* The caller may respond with the right answer, but the recognizer isn't sure enough to accept the response without confirming it first.

To handle all of these possible situations, speech-recognition systems often use these six types of prompts:

* Initial

* Retry

* Timeout

* Help

* Success

* Failure

Let's take a close look at each of these prompt types by going through the types of prompts that make up a typical call flow.

Initial Prompt

When a system enters in a particular state it may provide some information, but then, almost always, it asks a question such as "When do you plan to arrive?" The prompt played to the caller is called (logically) the **initial prompt** since it's the first thing the system says in a particular state/context. The recognizer then listens for the caller's answer.

Retry Prompt

If the recognizer hears something, but can't match the caller's utterance with the command vocabulary it is using in that context, then it will play a **retry prompt**. For example, if a caller says, "Uh, I guess I'm not sure" when the system is expecting to hear a date, such as "April 24th," the system would most likely not understand the utterance and then play a retry prompt to aid the caller.

We often use a retry prompt to clarify an idea with the caller, in the hope that by giving the caller another attempt he or she will understand how to answer a question correctly. For example, after hearing "Uh, I'd like to arrive on the last Saturday in April," an appropriate retry prompt might be an explicit statement, "I'm sorry I didn't understand. Please say the date you'd like to arrive. For example, you could say 'January 29th' or 'February 2nd.' Or for more information, say 'Help.'"

This retry prompt would help many callers, but not necessarily those who are saying the right thing but aren't being heard well—possibly (increasingly) because of bad connections on mobile phones. If the system still doesn't understand what the caller is saying, it might employ a second retry prompt, similar to the first one but with more or different information. For example, it might tell the caller, "I'm sorry, I still didn't understand. Say the date, or enter it, using touchtones. For example, you'd enter January 13th as zero, one, one, three. Otherwise, say 'Help' for more information."

Currently most speech-recognition engines are designed to reject a response after they've calculated that the caller's response is likely invalid. For example, if the caller answered the question "On which date?" with "The last Saturday in April," most likely the recognizer wouldn't understand that response. However, if the system were somewhat certain—but not certain enough—that it understood the answer, it might ask a confirmation question to verify the response, such as "I think you said April 2nd, is that correct?" This technique saves callers from repeating an answer in a case where the response the recognition engine heard is just below the threshold of acceptance.

Timeout Prompt

The system needs to determine whether the caller responded. If the recognizer doesn't hear anything, it will usually ask another question providing more information to the caller to elicit a response. This is called a **timeout prompt**.

To design timeout prompts we always need to ask ourselves, "Why wouldn't a person respond to this question?"

* Were they distracted and didn't hear or understand the whole question?

* Did they not know the appropriate words to use in response to the question?

* Did they not know the answer to the question?

* Did they not understand why they had to answer the question in the first place?

* Or did they not want to answer the question? Perhaps because they didn't want to reveal sensitive information?

So, for example, if a system asked, "When do you plan to arrive?" and fails to hear a response at all, it can provide a timeout prompt, such as "I'm sorry, I didn't hear you. Say the date that you plan to arrive, or for more information say 'Help.'" This new prompt provides a little more information about how to answer the question by instructing the person to say a date (rather than a relative time marker such as "After I get to Portland") and steers them to say "Help" if they need to find out more information about this question.

If callers' responses aren't heard twice in a state, a second timeout prompt can be used—often to instruct them on how to use touchtones or how to talk to a representative.

Help Prompt

Not to be confused with general help statements that explain how to use the system, the type of **help prompt** to which we're referring gives the caller assistance with a particular task in a particular situation. Designing a help prompt can be something of a challenge, because we, as designers, don't always know why callers would need help in a particular situation. So we have to make educated guesses by asking ourselves, "Why would callers not be sure how to proceed from here?"

Here are a few answers to that question.

* They didn't mean to be there in the first place.

* They changed their minds.

* There was something important missing from the original question.

* They didn't wait to hear the retry or timeout prompt messages.

We need to write our help prompt to address all of these possible needs.

Success Prompt

A **success prompt** is played when a caller has successfully exited the current state and is entering the next state. You may not choose to always use a success prompt, but if you do it can be as simple as "Got it," or more of an informative segue, such as "OK, now let's collect the last piece of information."

Failure Prompt

A **failure prompt** is played when callers have tried—and failed—to answer a question several times. They're obviously stuck and need to be either transferred to a "live" representative in a call center, or re-oriented (perhaps by being returned to the main menu). A typical failure prompt goes something like this: "Sorry, but it seems we're having problems. Let me transfer you to someone who'll be able to help. Hold on." In the case of a client without a call center behind the application, it might say "It looks like were having problems. Let's just take things from the top," then proceed to the main menu.

Often the designer can define this prompt once in the Design Specification and simply call for its use whenever a caller fails at a state. However, the designer should always look for situations in which this prompt may be inappropriate—or inadequate. For example, if the system has already collected information from the caller and can pass it along to a customer service representative, an appropriate prompt might be "Sorry, but it seems we're having problems. Let me transfer you to someone who'll be able to help and I'll pass along the information I've collected so far. Hold on."

THE ART OF WRITING PERFECT PROMPTS

The art of writing the perfect prompt is to convey ideas clearly and concisely. No extra words. No fuzzy language. A well-constructed prompt guides the caller to say *only* things the recognizer will understand. If a recognizer is able to understand almost everything that a caller might say in a particular context, then the prompt can be less directed. For example, a system might just say "Hello, and welcome to Thrifty Car Rental. What would you like?" Callers might say hundreds of thousands of things to answer this question, and thus the recognizer would have to be able to recognize most of them to be successful. Most recognizers don't work this way at the moment. If, however, the recognizer is looking for a particular word (such as a manufacturer of automobiles), the prompt must direct callers to answer specifically. For example, by having the prompt ask, "What's the automobile manufacturer?" instead of "What type of automobile?" we could minimize the chance that callers would say words such as "van" or "sedan."

In addition, prompt language must be consistent with:

* The original concept of the design

* The way the company expresses itself in other media

* The rest of the text spoken in the application

Writing Effective Initial Prompts and Commands/Command Phrases

Initial prompts must convey ideas clearly so callers can understand what they are expected to say. This doesn't mean that we need to provide callers with a long, drawn-out explanation at every turn of the dialogue. Once we establish that a particular calling population is comfortable with a speech-recognition system—and once we confirm that the caller has successfully answered some basic questions, like "Is that correct? Yes or no?"—then we can start to drop the "Yes or no" part and just ask the basic question.

As we've already discussed, it's important to be clear and consistent when writing prompts that present a list of options. For example, it may not be a good idea to have an initial prompt that says:

"Main menu. You can say 'Reports,' 'Exchange,' or 'Security.'"

The problem? There might be little or no context for the options—and the words themselves offer few clues. Both "Reports" and "Exchange" can be either nouns or verbs, and "Security" could refer to anything from data encryption to insurance coverage.

If, however, we rewrote the prompt so that all the selections were expressed in the form of imperative sentences that provide greater precision, callers could quickly understand the ideas—and their responses would also feel more conversational:

"Main menu. You can say 'Get the reports,' 'Make an exchange,' or 'Change my PIN.'"

Consistency is always important when designing prompts or when those prompts contain commands that the caller is to use later on. For example, the Wildfire Communications "voice-activated personal assistant," also called "Wildfire," uses the command "Describe it" to enable users to hear information about their phone messages (rather than listen to the actual message), such as the time the call arrived. But the clever thing about the design is that the user can say "Describe it" for any object—and Wildfire will tell the "header" information about that object. If a user said, "Describe it" while working with an e-mail message, Wildfire would tell the caller additional information about that message, such as who sent it, the subject of the message, and so on. By teaching the user a single command—and employing it consistently throughout the application—Wildfire makes it easy for its users to get more out of the system without learning new commands.

Designing Effective Retry and Timeout Prompts

How many retry and timeout prompts should a system give a caller before considering it a failure? I generally recommend presenting no more than two; anything more is likely to irritate a caller.

While it's sometimes acceptable to repeat the same prompt twice, often the designer will want to vary them to give the caller more information to help them answer the question correctly or get them back on track. As with help prompts, the best way to begin writing a retry or timeout prompt is by answering the question "Why would the caller not have said something valid at this point?" By considering all the possible answers to that question, we can write prompts that address most—if not all—of them. Many of the possible answers relate back to examining how the original prompt was written. For example, if we were designing a system for a motel by an interstate highway (frequented largely by travelers arriving by car or truck), we might assume that we needn't ask "Will you be parking a vehicle in our lot?" Instead, we'd skip ahead and ask, "What's the make and model of your vehicle?"

However, there will be at least a few people who won't be traveling to the motel by car or truck, but by bus, taxi, or maybe even on foot. The question "What's the make and model of your vehicle?" does not apply to them—and they wouldn't know how to skip the question. A retry or timeout prompt could circumvent this by saying "If you aren't bringing a vehicle, just say 'Let's go on.' Otherwise, what's the make and model of your vehicle?"

A similar situation arises when a caller embarks down a path they either didn't mean to take, or no longer wishes to take. A retry prompt can get the caller *unstuck* by including the phrase "...or if you don't want to be here say 'Main menu.'"

To be more foolproof, retry and timeout prompts should include further information about how to answer the question, but not so much information that it overwhelms the caller. Often the easiest way to do this is by providing a quick example. Instead of "Say the model year and make of your vehicle," the retry prompt could be "Say the model year and make of your car; for example, '1969 Mercedes-Benz.'" This tells the caller what format to use in answering the question.

An alternative is to suggest the touchtone equivalents to spoken answers, as in this example: "You can say 'Get the reports' or press 1, 'Make an exchange' or press 2, or say 'Change my PIN' or press 3." This approach is obviously better suited to questions with a limited number of possible responses—not hundreds, as in the vehicle example above.

Finally, all retry and timeout prompts should offer to direct callers to either the help prompt or a "live" representative, as in this example: "You can also say 'Help' or press the star key, or press zero for an operator."

Designing Effective Help Prompts

The help prompt is often the hardest to write, because the sequence of events leading up to the situation isn't tracked. Did the caller say "Help" immediately after hearing the initial question—or after two timeout and two retry prompts? We could be dealing with callers in greatly varying states of mind—from mildly confused to frustrated and irate.

When writing help prompts we again ask ourselves, "Why would anyone *not* know how to answer this prompt?" We need to ensure that the caller knows

* Why we're asking the question

* Where they are in the dialogue

* How (e.g., the format) to answer the question correctly

* How to get more help (e.g., talking to a "live" representative)

* How to escape this state to a "safety" zone (e.g., a main menu)

Here's a typical initial prompt and the help prompt that went with it.

Initial Prompt: At what airport, or city, are you picking up the car?

Help Prompt: Sometimes, rates and availability can depend on the location where you're picking up the car. Thrifty Car Rental has locations at airports throughout the U.S., Canada, and also in the rest of the world. *<pause>* To specify an airport, just say the name of the city and state you're interested in.

Note the use of the pause in that prompt. In this context that pause serves as a way to separate the background explanation from the command that the caller should react to—the pause gives a rhythmic break to regain the caller's attention.

Designing Effective Confirmation Prompts

Confirmations are an essential part of any design—even if they seem casual and unobtrusive—and they come in two varieties: explicit and implicit.

An **explicit confirmation** is when the system prompts the caller to answer a direct question before proceeding. For example: "OK, I think you'd like to buy 100 shares of Apple Computer, symbol AAPL, at the market price. Is that correct?"

This type of confirmation is best used when the risk of an unrecoverable error is present. To further prevent mistakes caused by misinterpretation of a caller's response, you can employ one of the following methods.

* The system can ask a "yes/no" question; for example, "Is that correct? Yes or no?"

* The system can ask the caller to say a PIN or a special password to confirm the transaction—or say "Cancel it" to cancel the transaction. This method assumes that the recognizer will not confuse the words "Cancel it" and the caller's password.

* The system can supplement the password confirmation by asking the caller to enter a number using the touchtone keypad to confirm or cancel. For example: "You have requested to purchase 100 shares of Apple Computer, symbol AAPL, at the market price. To confirm this transaction, press 1. To cancel, press 9." (If you use this method, attempt to avoid numbers that are close to each other on the keypad.)

* The system can disable the caller's ability to truncate the playing of a prompt by saying something or entering a touchtone number. If the system is programmed to disable this feature only during confirmations, it will prevent callers from accidentally assuming that the transaction is correct before hearing the entire confirmation statement. This method also reduces the liability of the company in the event of an error because it proves that the company did its best to ensure that the caller heard the entire statement before confirming it. It's worth noting that many companies save recordings of caller transactions to defend themselves in the event of any legal action—usually to defend themselves from callers who claim that the *machine made a mistake* when, in fact, the system actually did exactly what the caller requested.

WRITING PROMPTS FOR ELEGANCE, SPEED, AND VALUE

The difference between an adequate speech-recognition system and a great speech-recognition system lies in how the system asks questions and conveys complex information. Great systems do it with an elegance worthy of Audrey Hepburn; their meaning and impact are clear and immediate, and not a single word is wasted. The more elegant a system is, the more intuitively—and quickly—a caller can use it, and the greater value it offers to both clients and callers.

There are several mistakes commonly made that negatively affect the elegance, speed, and value of the system: providing unnecessary information, using ambiguous language, and not getting callers to focus on the essentials.

Unnecessary Information

Too often I hear systems that provide all callers with information that might only be useful to a small percentage of them. For example, I heard a cautionary message for U.S.-based services (used predominantly by U.S. residents who only make calls within the country) that provided information useful to only a small population. With some editing to protect the anonymity of the company, the prompt said something very similar to: "There could be a charge associated with using an access number if you call from the U.S. to another country such as, but not limited to, the former Soviet Union, Croatia, and Albania. Now, please tell me name of the city and state in which you live." Of course, sometimes disclaimers such as this are required by law, but they should only be played when necessary—not to every person who calls in. Not only is it long and distracting, but it also adds extra time to the call—and that means higher costs for the company paying for the toll-free line. Also, the disclaimer won't be effective if people are not going to listen to it, so it's in the best interest of the company to allow the designer to work with its legal team to aid in the writing of any required prompts so that the prompts are concise and intelligible while providing value to the listener and covering the company's liability.

Ambiguity in Language

In today's fast-paced world, we all use ambiguous or imprecise language as a kind of shorthand to save time and effort. Imprecise language causes the least negative impact in situations where a context can be clearly established and there is a high bandwidth of information exchange. An example is in face-to-face situations with people we know, where prior knowledge, body language, and vocal cues can fill in the blanks and add meaning to the words.

But it's a different story when one or more of those additional communication components—prior knowledge, body language, and vocal cues—are absent. The most extreme example is e-mail from an unknown person, where all three are absent. As every e-mailer knows, the intended meaning of written messages can easily be lost or misconstrued—particularly sarcasm and other forms of humor—which can lead to misunderstandings. Many e-mailers try to avoid this problem by adding **emoticons** and acronyms to their messages to help clarify their meaning:

"I know we hung out this morning but it feels like forever. :-) "

—where the set of *colon, dash, and close parenthesis* look like a smiley face turned 90 degrees counterclockwise.

Speech-recognition systems have the tremendous advantage of audio—which can include vocal cues, sound effects, and music—to add meaning to their outgoing communications. But because speech systems require clear answers from callers in order to function properly, it's essential that all prompts be as concise and unambiguous as possible.

That means we must carefully consider the language we use to convey ideas—even to the point of avoiding language that not only could be *misconstrued*, but even *misheard*. We can examine this situation by examining how people talk to each other. I was at a family gathering recently and overheard the following exchange among my Uncle Rob, Aunt Bobbie, and 22-year-old cousin Paul.

> UNCLE ROB: *Hey, Bobbie—I just found out Paul isn't dating a woman six years older than him—she's only six days older than him.*
>
> AUNT BOBBIE: *Well, that's certainly a relief.*
>
> COUSIN PAUL: *Uh, guys? You're both wrong. She's actually six months older than I am.*

The misunderstanding arose because my uncle misheard the age difference, only remembering the "six." Had my cousin said, "Yeah, she's half a year older than I am," there would have been less chance for confusion (and alarm on my aunt's part!). Using the phrase "half a year" instead of "six months" would limit the number of ways a listener could reasonably mishear the sentence. And none of those possible misheard phrases ("half a day," "half a week," or "half a year") would likely cause alarm—even to my Aunt Bobbie.

We can do the same thing when we write prompts for a speech-recognition system by understanding—and avoiding—the ambiguities of real-world conversations, and steering clear of language that could be misheard or misconstrued. Some systems try to avoid errors by repeating information back to the caller. This is a good idea when an answer needs to be precise—such as a stock trade—but unnecessary when a precise answer is not essential or can be easily modified later on.

GETTING CALLERS TO FOCUS ON THE ESSENTIALS

It's important for a system to use precise language, but other design components can make it easier for callers to comprehend and use the system—in particular, the order in which ideas are presented, and how those ideas are presented.

Presenting Information Clearly and Usefully

If we were designing a system that provides a warning message, we would want the system to alert the caller first before playing the message. Here's an example of a message that gets played when a single stock-trading account is accessed by more than one person at the same time. The system needs to alert the callers that this activity could be the result of an intruder.

> "Sorry, but the system is alerting me that there is another person accessing this account right now. I've alerted the system administrator, and for security protection, I'm disabling some functionality for this account (in case it isn't you on another phone), such as making a trade, reporting balances, and other things.
> However, you can still get real-time quotes and news updates."

By designing the system this way, we enable callers to decide whether they want to focus on the warning message and act upon it, or simply let it play so they can move on.

Presenting Information in a Meaningful Order

Some people apparently don't know the difference between essential and nonessential information. I'm sure we've all been at social gatherings where someone has trapped us in a corner with the promise of a fascinating anecdote, only to see it turn into a minute-by-minute, detailed account of his or her day. This forces us to try to filter out the unimportant data on the fly—which can be exhausting (and often fruitless). We feel like yelling, "Get to the point—or let me out of here!"

The same holds true for speech-recognition systems. Even if we think it's obvious what's important, we can't assume that callers will be able to filter those nuggets out of the rock pile. We can see how we modify our behavior in real life—as when I talk to my grandmother.

If I said to her:

> *"I walked past the yellow house on Main Street, and the first store on the right, which is a shoe store, has a pair of shoes in the window costing $45 that I think you'd really like."*

… she might give every detail of that account equal weight. She'd probably ask questions about the yellow house or its position on Main Street in order to clarify things in her mind, instead of focusing on the part I wanted her to—the inexpensive shoes. I should say:

> *"Grandma, I saw an inexpensive pair of shoes I think you would really like! If you're interested, just walk to the shoe store on the right side of Main Street (close to the yellow house) and look in the window for shoes marked $45."*

This construction uses the first sentence to set the context, and the second sentence to focus the details on how to achieve the goal. If Grandma didn't want a new pair of shoes, she could completely disregard the second sentence, knowing that it was only there to support the first.

Generally, the most important information should be presented first, and by *important* we mean information that is either the most critical or most descriptive of the context.

Here's an example of how a designer could make a mistake in a speech-recognition system.

"Flight 534 departing from Chicago O'Hare today, Thursday, July 5th from gate B9 in terminal 1, concourse B, is currently scheduled to depart at 8:45 P.M., on time."

In this example the most important information—the status and time—is buried deeply in the prompt. A better approach would be to guide the caller's focus to the most important information at or close to the beginning of the statement, hierarchically, so that if the information isn't immediately relevant to them they can ignore the rest of the statement.

"Flight 534 is scheduled to depart on time, at 8:45 P.M. from Chicago O'Hare today, Thursday, July 5th from terminal 1, concourse B, gate B9."

All callers need to know the status of the flight, and secondly, the departure time. Callers who are frequent flyers probably know the terminal number of the airline, and potentially even the concourse, then just read the gate information from the monitors. The information they need to know when calling (perhaps on their way to the airport) is whether the flight is on time. It's not good to bury important information deep inside the prompt, particularly if the plane is going to be delayed for four hours, in which event the gate information has a higher probability of changing.

These examples are a good way to understand some of the tricky elements of designing effective systems. However, it's necessary to get all the elements together to form the Design Specification from which the actual system will be produced.

SOME SUBTLETIES OF PROMPT WRITING

Some words and sentence constructs work better than others in speech-recognition systems—even when both are grammatically correct. Contrary to the protests of millions of elementary schoolchildren over the years, there are many reasons why we should speak using proper grammar—even in speech-recognition applications. The two biggest reasons? Precision and clarity. Grammatically correct language (unless it sounds extremely awkward) leaves less opportunity for misunderstanding.

I'm not overly pedantic about correct grammar and usage—it can be taken to ridiculous extremes—but a disregard for language betrays a certain sloppiness or lack of attention that reflects on a person or a company. For example, why do most supermarkets have checkout lines incorrectly labeled "12 items or less," instead of the correct "12 or fewer items?" "Fewer" has only one more letter than "less," so they're apparently not doing it to save space on their signs.

We can imagine a vacation-marketing survey system that asked questions about how people travel, and how they have enjoyed particular vacations booked through this company. If the system asked a series of questions about the person who accompanied the caller on a recent trip, the system might ask, "With whom were you?" This question, though grammatically correct, would confuse many people, and perhaps should be worded more colloquially as "Who were you with?"—to ensure that most people would understand the question.

Here are some rules of thumb that apply to virtually all U.S. applications.

"Want" Not "Wish"

Unless we're talking about systems run by genies or fairy godmothers, it's preferable to use "want" instead of "wish." People want answers, they don't usually wish for them. So instead of "Do you wish to search by date or by price?" use "Do you want to search by date or by price?"

"Say" Not "Speak"

"Enter or say your password" sounds a lot more natural than "Enter or speak your password." "Speak" sounds like a clinical term ("Yes, Doctor, the subject speaks whenever the bell rings. He also salivates.") The word "say" conveys a softer and more natural idea.

Contractions

Designers should use contractions in their prompts. Of course, when some people write text, they often do not use contractions, and it is perfectly correct. But try reading the sentence preceding this one out loud. It sounds as stilted and unnatural as the ending of this sentence, does it not? One of the great advantages of a speech-recognition system is its ability to create an affinity between the company and the caller—and it's harder to establish that sense of familiarity and comfort if the prompts are devoid of contractions, because most people simply don't talk that way. People are more likely to use—and enjoy using—a system if they feel there's a *regular* person on the other end of the line (even if that person happens to be a machine), and contractions help create that sense.

Word Order Matters

Often a sentence can be constructed in several ways, all of them grammatically correct. Which construct should we use? Whichever one more precisely conveys the idea. For example, the following two statements are both grammatically correct, but while the first correctly conveys the idea, the second could cause callers to start forming an incorrect mental model.

> **"If you don't think I'm going to get it right, say "Help.""**

> **"Say 'Help' if you don't think I'm going to get it right."**

The first sentence correctly indicates that in a situation where callers don't think the system is getting it right, they can say "Help" to (we would imagine) get a better understanding about the situation. In the second sentence, callers are instructed to say "Help" if—and perhaps only if—they think the computer won't get it right. If the word "Help" can be used in multiple contexts, we don't want to limit its use to only one of them.

The other reason why the first sentence is preferable to the second is that the caller's action—to say "Help"—is revealed *after* the system describes the circumstances that would prompt the action. This is a more logical sequence, and since callers' memories are short, it's always better to put the most important part of the instruction—to say "Help"—at the end.

Use of the Word "Just"

According to my dictionary, the word "just" has 13 meanings in English—6 as an adjective and 7 as an adverb. The differences in these meanings can be significant. For example, consider these two uses of "just."

	Meaning of "just"
Add just enough salt to give it flavor.	precisely, exactly
To get assistance, just say "Help."	simply, merely

In a speech system, we could have the system say either

"You say the search topic, and I'll look for something that sounds like it."

or:

"Just say the search topic, and I'll look for something that sounds like it."

The first sentence indicates that "anything you say" will be considered the search topic. The second statement is intended to say that the user simply needs to say a word to get the system going. However, a caller could misconstrue the meaning of "just" to be as it is in the first sentence above. Under that meaning, it sounds as if callers are required to know a precise search topic word (apparently from some top-secret list that the system isn't sharing) to get any results.

Use of "Want," "Like," "Can," and "May"

These words are often used interchangeably, but they actually have different meanings. Consider the following questions.

"Do you want me to read that back to you?"

"Would you like me to read that back to you?"

"Can I read that back to you?"

"May I read that back to you?"

The first question can evoke several reactions, depending on how it's said. It could sound as if it's urging the caller to listen, as in ""You *do* want me to read this to you, don't you?" However, it can also be directed to sound like the most neutral way to suggest the idea, as in "Do you want me to do this? Because I really don't care if I do or not."

By using "would," the second question sounds a little more formal and deferential than the previous statement, and it reinforces the personality of the system as someone eager to be helpful.

The third question is grammatically incorrect, substituting "can" for the correct "may." If taken literally, it means "Am I able to read that back to you?"—an irrelevant question. Beyond the grammar problem, it sounds as if the system really *wants* to read the statement back and is only waiting for the caller to give in and let it.

While "May I read that back to you?" is grammatically correct, it sounds as if the system is pleading with the caller to let it read the statement again. For some reason, "may" sounds too contrived to me. I have visions of a very proper British valet saying "May I draw your bubble bath now, your Lordship?" That's why I avoid it when designing any application.

Natural Language Shortcuts

A natural language shortcut allows callers to "skip" a bunch of steps by allowing them to provide several pieces of information to the application all in one sentence. The use of natural language shortcuts can be very effective, but only if the caller knows how—and where—to use them. For example, take a look at this exchange.

SYSTEM: **Where do you want to fly from?**
CALLER: *Boston.*
SYSTEM: **Where do you want to fly to?**
CALLER: *San Francisco.*
SYSTEM: **At what time?**
CALLER: *3 P.M.*

This exchange could be shortened considerably if the recognizer understood a natural language shortcut that allowed the caller to provide all the information (while still being able to understand just the first piece of information—in this case, the departure city).

SYSTEM: **Where do you want to fly from?**
CALLER: *From Boston to Los Angeles, at 3 P.M.*

This is a very convenient, quick, and natural option for people, but it is difficult for some recognizers to handle such a complex task. In fact, the recognition can be seriously compromised if the recognizer is expecting to hear only one token (a single piece of information, such as "Boston, Massachusetts") and instead hears a long string of several tokens (such as "Boston, Massachusetts to LAX, at 3 P.M."). People who tune these systems to improve recognition accuracy can do a lot to prevent recognition problems, but issues can still arise when we allow the use of a natural-language shortcut designed to listen for, and process several tokens while at the same time allowing the caller to simply indicate just one token of information. It's like a person ordering a pizza and just saying, "I'll have a pizza." The cook might expect that the person would indicate the size, and the toppings (even if it's just a "plain" pizza.) People can generally cope with this situation, but even real people get a little confused for a moment when they expect to hear more information than the person provides.

But what if a system does allow natural language shortcuts? How does it teach callers to take advantage of it? Is it best to tell all callers that they can "Just say their flight itinerary?" Or should that instruction only go to repeat callers who have a better chance—and probably a greater need and incentive—to memorize the structure that the system is looking for?

If the system has been programmed to identify callers and track their usage, it can be personalized to work in whichever way is best for each individual. For example, in a stock trading application, the system could have the caller work through a series of steps:

SYSTEM: **What kind of trade do you want to make? You can say "Buy," "Sell,"**
"Sell short,"—
CALLER: *Buy.*
SYSTEM: **How many shares do you want to buy?**

CALLER: *100.*

SYSTEM: **Of which security?**

CALLER: *Chemex Coffee Corporation.*

SYSTEM: **At what price?**

CALLER: *A limit price.*

SYSTEM: **Of what?**

CALLER: *88.*

SYSTEM: **OK, let me confirm that with you ....**

After the system has led the user through this process several times, it can be programmed to say the following (after the trade is completed).

> "Here's a hint: Next time, you can say the whole trade when I ask you the first question. So, for example, you could say, 'Buy 100 shares of Chemex Coffee Corporation at a limit price of 88'—all in one breath."

It's usually better to use callers' most recent trade as the example, because it personalizes and makes the experience more concrete and relevant to the callers—all of which will help them remember it the next time they call.

TOP FIVE GOOD TENETS FOR WRITING PROMPTS

1. State what the application will do and how it will work before engaging callers in conversation. The application needs to set the expectations of the caller and explain the role that it will serve. For example, a rate quote application that is made for people who have never spoken to a computer before would benefit from a phrase like "In a moment, we'll have a short conversation where you'll tell me what you want to ship, and I'll tell you how much it will cost." The caller knows that they'll need to talk to this computer and that the conversation will be short, and the system can provide a shipping rate quote. Sometimes the phrase can be as simple as

"Welcome to the United Airlines Flight Information System." This phrase is mainly intended to orient the user, and to prevent them from thinking that they can use the application for other services, such as buying a ticket or redeeming frequent flyer miles.

2. Design to the caller's level of knowledge at each state in the application, understanding that callers will learn terms and procedures as they use an application. Each state of an application should not be designed in isolation. As callers learn how to use a system, the system can take advantage of this to either shorten the length of the prompts, or to provide more information.

3. Use a consistent sentence structure for all commands within a single prompt (for example, "[VERB] the [NOUN]"). Other popular structures include

    [VERB] the [NOUN], as in: "'Make a payment,' 'Check balances,' and 'Calculate loan amount'"

    [NOUN/NOUN PHRASE], as in: "'Payments,' "Loan calculators,' and 'Balances'"

    [VERB], as in: "'Delete,' 'Play,' and 'Save'"

4. Ensure that all prompts should have a conversational tone in language and recordings to convey ideas clearly and simply. In general, a well-written prompt doesn't need to have a secondary explanation that attempts to simplify the concept in common parlance. The text should always be natural enough that further explanation of the concept provides *additional information* rather than simply restating the concept using simplified language.

5. Tell callers only as much as they need to know to make effective decisions—no more and no less.[1] Achieving the balance between too much and too little information can be tricky, but start by erring on the side of too little information so that brevity is achieved. Then examine the prompt to determine if there's something that absolutely cannot be left out.

---

1. To learn more about this see H. P. Grice, "Logic and Conversation," in *Syntax and Semantics*, Vol. 3, Peter Cole and Jerry Morgan, Eds. (San Diego: Academic Press, 1975) pp. 41–58.

TOP FIVE MISTAKES WHEN WRITING PROMPTS

1. Getting caught up in the details of the wording of an application before fully understanding its structure. This mistake can lead to lengthy rewriting of prompts if there becomes a need to change the structure of the application.

2. Writing overly verbose prompts.[2] People always consider the *context* when they evaluate a question. It is important to maintain a balance between clarity and brevity.

3. Repeating the initial prompt for the timeout and retry prompts. Timeout and retry prompts should provide additional information to clarify and guide the caller.

4. Using language not commonly found in conversation. For example, "won't" is almost always preferable to "will not."

5. Equating stilted language with formal language. It is possible to be both formal and simple. Instead of saying "You are required to provide your date of birth before we can proceed," you might choose to say, "We need to know your date of birth so that we can find your records."

WHERE WE'VE BEEN—WHERE WE'RE GOING

When designers finally finish getting their ideas on paper, they need someone to produce their work. That's where the producers come in. Showing someone a Design Specification is one thing, but actually using a real system is something else.

---

2. To learn more about this see Paul Grice, *Studies in the Way of Words* (Cambridge, MA: Harvard University Press, 1989) pp. 30–31.

SEVEN

PRODUCTION AND BRANDING

Imagination is the beginning of creation. You imagine what you desire, you will what you imagine and at last you create what you will.
—GEORGE BERNARD SHAW

At this point, the Design Specification has been completed. The designer and the client have agreed that the language in the document is appropriate, speech scientists have reviewed the design for recognition tasks that have been specified but might be hard for the recognizer to perform, and programmers have reviewed the document to ensure that the logic of the call flow is sound and programmable. It's now time to **render** the speech-recognition system—that is, to program and produce it.

There are many ways to program speech systems using any of a variety of pro-gramming languages and development environments available on the market. The most popular ones include touchtone development toolkits that have been modified to incor-porate the use of speech-recognition engines, as well as some built from the ground up. And while these programming environments all differ slightly, they all attempt to achieve the similar goals of providing a simple way to integrate a telephony environment with a speech-recognition engine and a database as well as a few other technologies. But when thinking about the production of the system, the only thing that really matters is that the completed program remains true to the design of the application, no matter which oper-ating system it's designed upon.

When designers also have to be programmers, they have been known to cut programming corners to make the application easier to implement and test. Sometimes this corner cutting doesn't affect the end product significantly. However, if done indiscriminately, it can undermine the elegance of certain design elements—and compromise the end result.

NOTES ABOUT IMPLEMENTATION AND PROGRAMMING

A typical speech-recognition system has a front end and a back end. The **front end** is where the system interfaces with the user (that is, what the caller actually hears and what the recognizer does). The **back end** is where it integrates with one or more databases (providing information to the caller in real time). Often the task of programming these components is handled separately—and concurrently—by a few developers; while one developer is programming the user interface, another can be integrating the system with the databases.

Once the system gets to the programming and implementation stage, there's usually very little for the interface designer to do until the development is complete and it's time to test the application. However, if the interface programmer completes work before the database programmer, there may be a need to create a temporary back-end database for testing purposes that simulates the workings of the real one. With this small database, which simulates the functionality of a real database, the interface programmer can test the system before the real database is hooked up. The designer may get involved at this point to advise the interface programmer on which types of data to load into the fake database.

For example, if we were designing a banking system, we might want to create a fake database consisting of several made-up accounts, each one representing a different type of bank customer. This would enable us to perform some **quality assurance tests** of the system against a broad range of callers and needs as defined in the Requirements Specification. Quality assurance testing is performed to verify that all the code works as intended. This testing is not the same as **usability tests**, which ensure that the target population can use the system and enjoy using it (see Chapter 8).

After everyone has successfully completed and tested their work, all that remains is to load the prompts (or audio files) that have been recorded by the designer and connect the system to the telephone lines (another task that is often also handled by a separate expert).

PRODUCTION

When we talk about the **production** of a speech-recognition system, we're referring not to the programming, but rather to the design of the audio portion of the system—in other words, everything the callers hear when they phone in. Any application that talks to people requires, at minimum, some form of audio source that asks questions and makes statements; for example, "What is your account number?"

PROMPT CREATION—TEXT-TO-SPEECH AND RECORDED VOICES

There are two ways to create audio prompts. One method is to record a real person, called a **voice talent**, saying phrases, while the other is to use text-to-speech (TTS) software that converts text stored in a digital form (for example, an e-mail message) to a spoken utterance, in real time. TTS is generally used to read dynamic information in a cost-effective manner that otherwise would be difficult or impossible to prerecord, for example, the daily news or the weather. There are two types of popular TTS engines— those that synthesize the sound, **formant TTS**, and those that take thousands of small pieces of prerecorded human-speech and concatenate them, or string them, together, called **concatenative TTS**. The following are the primary differences among the three methods (recorded phrases and the two types of TTS) of producing the audio files.

- Recorded prompts sound great and convey the most precise meaning, since voice talents can vary every aspect of how they speak according to the desired direction. However, each prompt takes up disk space, though not a large enough amount as to be much of an issue.

* Formant TTS engines sound the worst; they don't sound like any particular voice talent since they generate the speech signal from scratch using a noise generator and a series of filters to change the noise to make it sound like speech. However, they can sometimes be a good choice because they require very little computing power, disk space, or memory.

* Concatenative TTS engines, when built properly, are able to sound nearly like the person from whom the audio files were recorded (allowing seamless blending between the recorded prompts and the TTS-generated ones), though they can't convey the rich meaning that the recorded prompts can. However, these systems require faster computers and much more disk space and memory.

Most often it's a good idea to use recorded prompts, since they will sound the most natural and the total time to record the prompts is generally a fraction of the total time of development. I don't advocate only using TTS prompts for an entire application, because that method could compromise the ability to express the endless amount of variation that the human voice can produce to convey particular thoughts.

The preferred and more traditional method is to record a real person—the voice talent—saying phrases that are recorded and stored digitally in a computer, with each phrase saved as a unique file and played to the caller as appropriate. Even though callers know that they're not listening to a live person, they are much more comfortable interacting with something that sounds more like a fellow human being[1] and less like the somewhat emotionally removed HAL 9000 from *2001: A Space Odyssey*.

Production of effective audio prompts requires three tasks.

* Casting—choosing the appropriate voice talent

* Directing—guiding the voice talent in how to say the words

* Concatenative recording—ensuring that the phrases spoken by the voice talent are captured and can be joined together for smooth playback

---

1. See Byron Reeves and Clifford Nass, *The Media Equation: How People Treat Computers, Television, and New Media Like Real People and Places* (New York: Cambridge University Press, 1996), pp.106–107.

CASTING

Casting the right voice is one of the most important tasks in creating a successful speech-recognition system. The right voice talent must be appropriate for the application and reflect the overall brand of the client. A large bank might want to cast a voice talent for their advertisements that possesses a strong, masculine quality such as Charlton Heston. However, his voice *may not* be appropriate for their speech applications because it might sound too rough or intense. The right voice may have similar hallmarks to Heston's, but might sound more approachable and friendly. (See the section "Choosing the Voice of the Brand" later in this chapter for a more detailed discussion of this topic.)

One way to start the casting process is to call local recording studios or casting companies and ask for a demo tape or CD of several voice talents. It is reasonable to ask the talents to read a script that you have prepared so that you can hear the voice talents saying the exact text that would be used for a system. Listening to these samples will help narrow the pool of candidates. But listening to an audio sample will not reveal what it's like to work with a particular voice talent—or how that person will sound reading the actual audio prompt script. So it's usually a good idea to audition the voices personally.

Typically, it only takes about 30 minutes to audition a prospective voice talent, having them

- Understand what they're reading

- Understand the context in which it will be heard

- Read several types of prompts that are representative of various parts of an application

For the audition, you should prepare a short script that includes either actual system prompts or—if casting is done earlier in the design process—made-up prompts similar to the ones that will be in the completed system. These can include basic prompts, such as:

"Welcome to Cool Startup, Incorporated." (To be spoken warmly)

"Please enter or say your PIN number." (To be spoken casually)

"I'm sorry, but this account has been temporarily disabled." (To be spoken sincerely)

It's also a good idea to include prompts that follow each other in a list, such as

"Thirty."

"Forty."

"Fifty."

… and so on.

By having the voice talent read several prompts like these sequentially, you can determine whether the talent (either intuitively or with direction) can speak each number using the same tone and frequency, or pitch. That's important to know, because if the pitch of the talent's voice rises at the end of each word during the actual recording—as if they were reading a list to someone—it will make it harder for the recording engineer to concatenate and rearrange the numbers later. It's best to have a voice talent who can keep his or her volume, tone, and pitch consistent on prompts such as these.

You should also take some time during the audition to direct each voice talent and monitor their reactions. This can help you gauge how easy—or difficult—it would be to work with that person during a potentially long, painstaking, and repetitive recording session.

Cost is a key factor to consider while casting for voice talent. Most voice talents—both union and nonunion—charge by the hour. Union talent is generally more expensive, and their contracts can include stipulations and restrictions about working conditions, such as overtime charges, travel expenses, and so on. However, membership in an actor's union usually implies a higher level of professionalism and experience, both of which help to ensure a fast and successful recording session. Nonunion talent is generally—but not always—less expensive, because they set their own rates. And nonunion talent can be just as good as union talent. However, be sure that the voice talents have the skills and experience necessary to do this exacting work. In either case, a local recording studio or casting company can provide a more complete understanding about pricing for each.

What about amateur talent? Well, there are occasionally natural talents who sound just perfect and can learn on the job, but such people are few and far between. And as we're about to see, there's more to being a successful voice talent than just having a nice voice and being able to read.

DIRECTING VOICE TALENTS

Directing voice talents requires a great deal of concentration and attention to detail. Just as on stage or in movies, even the most seasoned, professional talents need direction to deliver the best performance. It's up to the designer to articulate how the application should feel—and consequently, how the voice talent should sound.

Should the talent affect a produced, *professional* sound? Or should he or she speak more casually—for example, not hitting any ending consonants (like the last "t" in "that") so they sound more conversational? Even within these general directions there are sub-categories, including

* Speed (how quickly the words are spoken)

* Range (the actual notes in the phrases)

* Duration of pauses between words and phrases

* Elongation of words (when people want to sound reluctant, they often stretch out some of the words, as in "Welllll, juuuust this once….")

Keep in mind that the entire application doesn't need to be totally consistent in terms of the style of direction. Sometimes it's a good idea to mix in casual phrases between the important phrases to add color to the application. This can also provide a mental respite to listeners as they think about what they've been doing. For example, a stock trading application may use a lightly humorous, off-the-cuff phrase like "You don't need to remember any commands—I'll make sure you know what you're doing before I stop providing hints." If the talent is directed to deliver this line in a slightly tongue-in-cheek way, it can help relax callers.

Conversely, some *casual* applications may benefit from the adoption of a more formal tone for certain lines or phrases to provide added emphasis and ensure that the caller pays close attention. Here's an example from an airline application: "Since your luggage has been located, it *will* be sent to the address you provided us on the claim form. If you *don't* want it sent there, say 'Agent' and we'll change the address right away."

A great way to get voice talents into the right frame of mind for the recording is to ask them to visualize a place or an environment that conveys the feeling of the application. This is not as strange as it may sound. After all, when people write reviews of music, they often do so using art terminology (describing the *color, form*, or *texture* of a musical performance) and art is often described musically (using words like *rhythm, dissonance*, and *loudness*).

I once directed the recording for an application that was going to be used by a very large and broad spectrum of people worldwide. I told the voice talent to imagine a Monet painting called "Entrance to the Village of Vetheuil in Winter,"[2] which depicts a dirt road fading into the distance. In the painting, a few people walk down the road surrounded by fields with a couple of houses in the distance. Overhead, the clouds of a winter storm have just broken to reveal a glow of orange afternoon light.

This imagery helped set the idea of a cooler, relaxed pace. But I also wanted the voice talent to imagine that he and the caller were walking down the dirt road in a purposeful yet unhurried way. It helped the voice talent to find a particular range in his voice that felt *comfortable* to him and would feel *comforting* to the caller. This use of guided imagery is a great way to elicit a good voice performance, and the imagery need not be fine art—or any art at all. To get a voice talent in the right frame of mind to record for a super-hip voice portal application, for example, you might suggest imagining an evening among beautiful people at the coolest nightclub or disco in town. What's right is whatever works.

Often, the same voice talent will sound very different depending on who's directing him or her. This can become noticeable when a company goes back to record additional prompts for an existing application. If the voice talent is the same but the director is different, the resulting prompts may not match the earlier ones. Sometimes this effect can

---

2. The painting is part of the permanent collection of the Museum of Fine Arts in Boston.

be mitigated if the voice talent listens to several of the previous recordings and tries to copy them; however, this rarely is a substitution for consistent direction. Once the voice talent is in the right mindset, it's time to start recording.

Usually, the most important phrases in the application are the initial prompts that every caller will hear—the "welcome" prompt, for example, or the first questions asked. I highly recommend recording all of these high-level prompts in the first session—before any other prompts. This enables the voice talent to retain the context of the recording and maintain a consistent tone.

That means you should select the most common, logical path for the majority of callers, and put all the prompts from that path at the beginning of the script. Then, when the voice talent is recording the phrases that have been logically arranged, he or she can gain an understanding of how the finished product will sound to callers—and can start thinking about how to voice it properly. Often, when prompts are arranged in this way, the voice talents themselves will know enough to spot and correct some of their own errors before the director can do so.

THE ART OF RECORDING PROMPTS

Proper recording of audio prompts is key to creating an effective speech-recognition system. Once the voice talent has been cast and the prompt script finalized, it's time to get to a recording studio and ensure that all the words are spoken and recorded to express the right ideas in the right way with the right feeling.

As the director of the recording session, the designer must ensure that all of the following elements are captured correctly.

Pronunciation	Are the words pronounced properly?
Articulation	Are the words clear and intelligible?
Intonation	Is the pitch of each prompt correct for its context?
Expression	Are the meaning of the words being conveyed?
Emotion	Are the ideas behind the words being conveyed?

If any of the above elements are *off*, unexpected errors can occur later on. Mistakes aren't always immediately obvious, either; often the difference between the right prompt and the wrong prompt can be quite subtle. For example, let's say we're recording a prompt for an airline flight information system. One of the prompts is

"Would you like the gate information for an international flight?"

Looks simple and unambiguous, right? But there are at least three possible ways to interpret that line. If a voice talent was asked to record the prompt without any specific direction about its context, he or she might assume that the system was simply offering information to the user—and might, accordingly, read it as a fairly *flat* and simple question.

But what if we actually wanted the prompt to distinguish "gate information" from some other type of information, such as the arrival time or baggage claim location? In that case, the word "gate" should be emphasized.

"Would you like the *gate* information for an international flight?"

Or perhaps we want to distinguish international flights from domestic flights. In that case, the correct reading would be

"Would you like the gate information for an *international* flight?"

By recording the prompts with the right emphasis, you can ensure that the system asks questions to convey the desired intent.

An effective speech-recognition system should create an affinity between the client and the caller. That's why pronunciation can be important. Generally, callers want to hear words pronounced the way that the caller pronounces them. And even if the voice talent has no discernable regional accent, he or she might pronounce a word—often a place name—differently from the local population simply for lack of knowledge. For example, imagine if a local bank in Oregon got acquired by a larger bank, and the new bank's speech-recognition system had a prompt offering branch location information for "Ore´-uh-gahn" instead of "Ore´-uh-gin." Bank customers in that state, perhaps already concerned that their bank is no longer locally owned, might feel even more alienated by the perceived mispronunciation. This can also happen (and would be more likely to happen) if the voice talent had to read a list of a few hundred cities, not all of which were familiar to the talent.

Of course, not all prompts need such careful attention. But there is indeed a direct relationship between the effectiveness of the system and the attention paid to how each prompt is spoken. Even very good voice talents—people who have been working in the industry for 30 years—won't necessarily understand how to say a particular prompt, because the prompts are often recorded out of context and out of order.

Imagine recording the phrase "Since today is a national holiday…." on the first day of the recording sessions, and then, three days later the designer were to record all the prompts that fit into the next position, for example, "… the bank's branches will be open from 8 A.M. until noon." The result could be the audio equivalent of a ransom note composed from cutout newspaper and magazine letters; everything's there, but nothing fits together well.

It is the job of the designer/director to get the voice talent to convey not only the correct meaning of the prompts, but also the ideas and feelings behind the prompts. Does the client want to present itself as caring and compassionate? Precise and efficient? Friendly and informal? Conservative and formal? The voice talent needs to know in order to effectively convey the ideas and feelings behind the prompts. Knowing how to get a voice talent to produce the right quality of sound is something that all directors for all media learn by doing. There are many techniques: some directors describe the intent of the prompt to the voice talent and then keep refining their descriptions, while other directors (like me) ask the voice talent to mimic and imitate the way I say it, until the talent gets the hang of it and can extrapolate how to say the subsequent phrases with far less directing.

OTHER THOUGHTS ON DIRECTING

Although it may serve the purposes of some brands to feature a voice with near-perfect articulation—perhaps an English voice talent for British Airways—voices don't need to over-articulate anything, except the most important words and concepts. Why? Because normal articulation sounds natural and is still easily understood by callers. Have you ever heard a fast-food worker say, "Would you like fries with that?" and punch every syllable plus the ending "t" in "that?" Of course not. Usually they just mumble something like "Wouldja like fries witha?"—where the words "with" and "that" run together. Even the most persnickety speakers say, "I'd like anapple," rather than pausing between the words "an" and "apple." This is called **connected speech**, and when it's used over the phone, it sounds just as natural and conversational as in real life. The more natural the sound, the more at ease and attentive the listener will be to what matters most—the meaning of the words.

CONCATENATIVE PROMPT RECORDING

Concatenative prompt recording refers to the recording of a voice talent saying particular words that will later be spliced together. Let's use the phrase "I'll transfer 50 dollars from your checking account to your savings account" as an example.

Most touchtone systems deliver this phrase poorly—here's an example. (Read this aloud to understand what I mean.)

> **"Transferring. Fifty, dollars. From your, savings. Account. To your, checking. Account."**

It sounds stilted and artificial—particularly when we hear the first instance of "account" where the system, using the only recording it has of "account," sounds as if it is finished its thought. This problem is generated from designers who seek to do the minimal amount of intellectual work by recording one version of each word that they'll use without regards to context.

If we examine the word "account" when spoken naturally by a person, we see that it is used in two different contexts: when it refers to the originating account and will be followed by some more information, and at the end of the sentence (when it refers to the destination account).

When we speak, we all vary the intonation of our words or phrases to suit their context. In audio prompt recordings, we refer to three basic types of intonation.

* **Rising**—when the pitch of the word or phrase rises at the end, as in the beginning of a sentence.

* **Medial**—when the pitch of the word or phrase remains steady, as in mid-sentence.

* **Falling**—when the pitch of the word or phrase descends at the end, as in the end of a sentence.

If there were five types of accounts, the bad touchtone example requires the recording of ten prompts (plus all the numbers).

"Transferring" / "< ... list of numbers ... >" / "dollars" / "from your" / "checking"/
"savings" / "money market" / "brokerage" / "retirement" / "account" / "to your" /

The system can be greatly—and easily—improved to sound like this (again, read it aloud)

"Transferring, 50, dollars from your checking account, to your money market
account."

by only recording 11 prompts—the right 11 (plus the numbers). The basic idea is to record larger phrases with regard to the context in which they'll be played, and then program the application to concatenate them correctly. We only have to create two recordings for each type of account: one using a medial intonation when it is the *originating account,* and one with falling intonation when it is the *destination account.* For five types of accounts, here is the recording list.

"Transferring"

"< ... list of numbers ... >" (e.g., "31," "32," "33," "34," and so on)

"dollars, from your checking account" / "dollars, from your savings account" /
"dollars, from your money market account" / "dollars, from your brokerage
account" / "dollars, from your retirement account"

"to your checking account." / "to your savings account." / "to your money market account." / "to your brokerage account." / "to your retirement account."

Remember the old TV game show *Password?* The object of the game was for players to get their partners to say a word by giving them clues. One common tactic was to say the beginning of a common phrase using a medial tone in order to get the partner to complete the phrase. Player A might say "Hammer and ...." (with a leading tone to the word "and") to get player B to finish the phrase—"nail."

But it's not just whole words that can be concatenated to form phrases. Parts of words can also be concatenated, most often when the application calls for numbers. The minimal number of recordings to express North American formatted telephone numbers is ten (one recording for each digit, 0 to 10). However, the result sounds like this.

"Six. One. Seven. Four. Two. Eight. Four. Four. Four. Four." (with each "4" sounding exactly the same)

To achieve a significantly more natural sound in an application that uses numbers, we would want to record a total of 30 prompts—each of the numbers 0 to 9 in all three intonations: rising, medial, and falling.

This technique would enable the system to concatenate the prompts so that a number like 555 ("five, five, five") sounds like a complete thought, with a rising sound to the first five, a medial sound to the second five, and a falling sound to the final five. And while it will sound less "robotic" than the minimalist approach, most listeners will be able to detect that the numbers have been pasted together (unless the recording and the splicing are done carefully).

Alternatively, it is possible to achieve exceptional, natural-sounding quality, but it requires the recording of 1,200 prompts—recording every complete three-digit prompt from 000 to 999, plus two sets of two-digit prompts (from 00 to 99), one rising and one falling. This means that phone numbers like "(617) 428-4444" will be played from audio files that are recordings of someone saying the complete phrases: "617," "428," "44" (rising), and "44" (falling). Piece them together and it sounds totally natural—but the obvious cost is the amount of time to record the additional 1,170 phrases.

SOME METRICS AND TECHNICAL NOTES

How long will the recording process take? It varies, depending on many factors. But a good director, using software that makes it easy to record a large number of prompts quickly, along with professional, experienced voice talents, can record about 200 prompts per hour. (This average includes every kind of prompt, from short numbers to long instructions.) That's important to consider, because time can be a major cost factor. As of this writing, many nonunion talents charge from $100 to $400 per hour, while union talents charge about $1,300 per hour—not including studio time and casting costs. Most directors can assume that a mid-sized application (one designed to deliver flight information or a simple home banking application) requires about 14 hours of directing. The number of hours will vary a lot, depending on how good the voice talent is, how good the director is, and how many mistakes need to be corrected in subsequent recording sessions. So a budget between $3,000 and $5,000 is reasonable for nonunion talent, while a budget of $12,000 to $18,000 is more likely for union talent.

When recording voice talents, it's always better to make the recordings digitally in a high-quality format —by recording them directly to a computer or other digital media— even though the final product will be played over a low-bandwidth device (the phone). There are two reasons for this. First, it allows the recordings to be repackaged for other uses, such as TV and radio spots or presentations. Second, recording and saving the prompts in a high-quality format enables them to be **down sampled** (changed to another format of lesser quality) in many different ways for use by any speech-recognition system. This minimizes any loss of quality that may occur if, for example, a designer recorded the prompts in a low-fidelity proprietary format. Doing so would prevent the designer from getting the best quality when those audio files were then imported into a different software environment.

Finally, what happens if the recording session is completed—and later it's discovered that the designer needs to record one or two minor prompts? This may necessitate setting up another studio session with the voice talent at a substantial minimum cost. However, many voice talents have their own home-recording systems—and with today's digital technology, even a home system can deliver high-quality audio. In that case, the designer can simply ask the voice talent to record the missing prompts for a small fee and forward the files via e-mail.

AUDIO ICONS

Getting the recorded prompts sounding right is critical, but there are other sounds that can be used in an application besides the spoken word. **Audio icons** are short sounds— for example, a *blip*, a *swoosh*, or a set of tones—that may or may not have words spoken over them. Some well-known examples are the three tones associated with NBC radio and TV, the opening chord that sounds when a Macintosh computer is started up, or the four-note phrase that accompanies "Intel Inside" in all Intel radio and TV spots. These usually short sounds can add much to the feel and user experience of an application.

What Audio Icons Can Do

Audio icons serve a number of purposes. When callers hear a welcoming phrase and an audio icon (for example, "Welcome to FedEx RateFinder <audio icon>"), they are immediately informed that (a) they are not speaking to a live person (nobody I know picks up the phone, says "Hello," and plays a music chord); and (b) this is a well-produced, *professional-sounding* system.

But that's not all. If the speech system is a replacement for an older (perhaps touch-tone) system, the audio icon alerts the caller to that fact—without subjecting them to annoyingly long-winded statements like "Please listen to all the menu selections before choosing one, as our options have changed." (I've been known to call back into those systems to check if their options have changed. Usually I find that they keep that phrase in there for months ... or longer.)

Perhaps most importantly, audio icons can also aid in the branding of a service, product, or company. By repeating a unique sound used by the company in its commercials (for example, the Sprint "pin drop"), the audio icon conjures up a vision of the brand in the mind of the caller, reinforcing and strengthening that brand identification. Audio icons can even help create the *feel* of an application. For example, if we were to create a system for a manufacturer of large machines, we might choose to use a set of industrial sounds to underscore the identity of the company.

Audio icons can also act as **anchors**, helping users locate where they are in an application. If we created an application with a main menu, we could program the system to play an audio icon whenever a caller was at that place. Eventually, as callers learn to associate the audio icon with the main menu, the system could even stop saying "Main menu," using *only* the audio icon to orient the user.

And it doesn't have to stop there. For applications that are going to be used repeatedly by the same caller, designers can employ a series of audio icons throughout an application to remind callers where they are. When callers hear the same sound repeated in the same place in an application, they can quickly learn to associate the two—a helpful method to let callers know where they are in an application without having to listen to lengthy spoken text.

Some Limitations of Audio Icons

One caveat. We shouldn't go overboard using audio icons. Audio icons can enhance the brand and improve the user experience—but add too many and the entire experience becomes unpalatable. If an audio icon is used at the beginning of a prompt, taking up a couple of seconds before the spoken prompt starts, and if that audio icon doesn't serve as an anchor point to orient the caller, then eventually the caller will become frustrated with the system because the system is noticeably taking up the caller's time but not providing value to the caller. Also, if there are a lot of audio icons sprinkled throughout the application, the interruptions can erode the conversational flow of the system.

The only real limit to the use of audio icons is a technological one. The conventional telephone transmission system is unable to carry bright, high-frequency and deep, low-frequency tones. In fact, the telephone frequency range is only 300 Hz to 3,400 Hz, while the range most people can hear is approximately 30 Hz to 20,000 Hz. I once had an audio-icon producer make a set of audio icons. One that I particularly liked was a cartoon sound effect to accompany the wave of a magic wand. I thought it would be a great sound to be played underneath a "transferring to representative" message. However, when I tried it out on a real system, I couldn't hear a thing. The sound's frequencies exceeded the range of the telephone.

You can prevent this embarrassment by avoiding very high or very low tones. But just to be sure that any audio icon will sound right in an application, you should always listen to the audio icon as it will sound on the phone. It's easy to create that listening experience by using a simple sound-editing program to emulate how the audio would sound over a phone line, since the tiny speaker in the phone can't reproduce sounds like a good stereo system can.

Most audio files are made and delivered to the system designer in high fidelity or near *CD quality* sound (either 44.1 Hz or 22.05 Hz). Using a sound-editing program (several of which are available via free Web downloads), the designer can *down sample* the sound to 8,000 Hz and play it. If the audio quality of the down-sampled icon sounds awful, don't be alarmed (yet.) Often, audio that sounds pretty bad via speakers or headphones sounds surprisingly "OK" over the phone. This time the reason isn't technical; it's because our ears are so accustomed to hearing low-fidelity sound over the phone that our brains actually *fill in* the missing information (for example, the crisp *s* sound in "Christmas"). Result? It appears to sound better than it actually is.

BRANDING

Our discussion of audio icons leads to one of the primary uses of such icons: **branding**, the unique identity that a company, product, or service holds in the mind of the consumer. Most clients looking for a speech-recognition system have an application need in mind; they're not thinking about how that system will function as an extension of their brand. The telephone is a communication medium, just like TV and radio. In fact, the telephone can even be considered superior to those other media because it offers true, one-to-one interactive communication—and best of all, you can count on customers having a phone. Clients need to understand that—and to realize that a speech-recognition system can be as effective a marketing vehicle as any radio spot or TV commercial.

Branding Basics

Brand identity allows similar companies to compete—and to market themselves to different groups of people. For example, the brand identity of Volvo automobiles is *safety*.

Over the years, Volvo has invested millions of dollars promoting the safety of its cars. It doesn't really mean a Volvo is a safer form of transportation than any other, but it does mean that people may choose to buy a Volvo—without having done any comparative research—because they've been led to believe they are safe vehicles. That's effective branding.

Likewise Apple Computer. Apple has distinguished its products in the PC market-place by emphasizing their ease of use, innovation, and great design. That's the essence of its branding—which is why we don't see iMac commercials that stress processing speed or other technical attributes.

FedEx is another great example of a strong brand identity. FedEx has become so synonymous with the delivery of packages that "absolutely positively" have to be there the next day, that people now use the brand name as a verb—"I need to FedEx this pack-age tonight"—even if they're using a different carrier! In doing so, FedEx has joined the small club of brands whose names are used interchangeably with the product category, just like Kleenex (tissues) and Xerox (copiers).

Having a strong brand is a powerful competitive advantage—but it can't be taken for granted. Smart companies continuously protect and reinforce their brand identities via every communication medium at their disposal.

Many companies have great Web sites, strong marketing collateral, compelling advertising, top-notch customer service representatives—and really bad touchtone phone systems. Perhaps they don't care. Perhaps they don't think of their phone systems as a marketing channel. Perhaps they don't even realize how powerful a tool their phone sys-tems can be. Whatever the reasons, these companies are missing out on an important opportunity—to strengthen their customer relationships, improve customer satisfaction, and build their brands among the people who matter most.

Most companies pay a great deal of attention to how their brands are communicated in their advertising and marketing literature. But these are outbound communications with no direct, interactive connection to the customer. An advertisement can be ignored or turned off. A brochure can be left unread. But when a customer calls a company, it is one of the most direct and personal contacts that company will ever have with a customer.

Contrary to popular perception, customers don't always object to using an automat-ed system. In fact, they often prefer the anonymity it provides for more private transactions, such as selecting a PIN for a brokerage system. (Do you really want that customer care representative knowing that your password is as easy as 1, 2, 3, 4?) Telephones are also ubiquitous—unlike Internet access—enabling customers to call from anywhere at any time. A speech system can handle many types of interactions—from sales to service—and it can be customized to reinforce the company's brand at the same time.

By taking branding into consideration from the beginning, companies can ensure that their phone system handles customers the right way all the time—in a manner that's consistent with its brand identity.

Branding over the Phone

There are two primary questions to answer when contemplating how a company's brand should be manifested over the phone.

* What kind of brand does the company have (or want to have)?

* What role will the application play in expressing the brand?

The answer to the first question is sometimes obvious—particularly for companies that already have strong brands. We can imagine how a speech-recognition system for, say, the Gerber baby food company might sound (or might *not* sound). I would imagine that we'd all agree that it shouldn't sound like an aggressive ruffian.

But sometimes it's not as simple as determining what it *shouldn't* be like. Often you have to dig a little deeper, especially if a company's branding is based more on its aspirations than its current reality. You can begin to get an accurate depiction of a company's messaging by collecting as much corporate communications material as possible—from brochures to videos to press releases. In addition, talking to the company's marketing executives will provide further insight into the intent of those marketing messages. Often companies can supply internal documents or research materials that discuss the company's positioning in the marketplace.

The answer to the second question will vary greatly, depending on the company and the application. The application might be just one of the company's several customer service channels, such as a flight information system for a large airline. Other times, the application *is* the brand—for example, a voice portal. A voice portal has no customer service representatives behind it, and no real product other than the information that callers receive. While the flight information line needs to have a personality that is helpful and reflects the brand of the rest of the company, the voice portal can (and probably should) be more entertaining, fun, and upbeat. Why? Because the portal may also be designed to sell products and services…and who wants to be sold experiential entertainment consumer goods by a sad sack? Even a casket company doesn't want to sound morose over the phone—professional, but certainly not downbeat.

In the process of digesting all this information, you should begin to develop a sense of the brand's *personality*—and how it should be expressed over the phone.

Choosing the Voice of the Brand

Choosing the voice of a brand can be a challenge, since it involves considering not only the gender of the voice (and any accompanying stereotypes), but also the type and texture of the voice. An important question to ask is "Who should the voice personify?" Should it be the voice of the very best customer care representative in the company? Or a voice like the one featured in the company's TV and radio spots?

There are two ways to think about the personality behind the voice.

* The feeling that the voice conveys—no matter what they are saying

* The character or social environment evoked by the voice

We've all heard voices that sound unusual or grating or smooth or sexy. These voices convey a particular feeling—no matter what they are saying. I imagine James Earl Jones sounds authoritative even when he's ordering a pizza. Melanie Griffith still has a naive, teenage quality to her voice—even though she's been an adult for decades. And who can listen to Lauren Bacall without visualizing a luxury Park Avenue apartment—even when she's selling cat food!

Designers need to consider these impressions when they choose a voice. You probably wouldn't select Melanie Griffith as the voice of Dodge Ram Trucks, nor would we be likely to hire Rosie O'Donnell to record audio prompts for the National Gallery of Art. And James Earl Jones might be a disaster as the voice of Blind skateboards.

But when the voice and the company are matched—like Tom Selleck and AT&T for the "You Will" ad campaign—the designer's branding work practically takes care of itself. In this case, the quality of the advertisements was futuristic in concept and look but very accessible in tone and text. Selleck's voice was warm and conversational, which could easily lend itself to be used in a speech-recognition system.

Advertising Voices

Sometimes the casting of the voice can be easy, especially if the company has an existing advertising campaign that features a recurring character or a consistent voice-over (not that a designer would always want that particular voice). A good example of this is Bank of America TV advertisements. In one series of advertisements they used a child with an unusually raspy but obviously young voice. A designer might choose to imagine how this child will sound when he's grown up a bit, and then cast a voice that is a little raspy but also has other qualities that reflect other aspects of the company. The designer could cast someone in his late 20s to early 30s to keep the "feel" youthful, but with added "depth" to convey trust.

Just because a company has an identifiable commercial spokesperson doesn't mean the designer should use that same voice in the speech-recognition system. Because of the limitations of telephone audio, some TV voice talents may not sound as good—or even recognizable—on the phone. The designer should feel free either to choose a different voice with similar characteristics or to try something completely different. If we were casting a voice for Verizon, for example, we might avoid their spokesperson, James Earl Jones, entirely and go with a female voice talent—akin to a TV co-host. The only criterion that matters is to choose a voice with a personality that works in accordance with the company brand and complements the commercial spokesperson.

WHERE WE'VE BEEN—WHERE WE'RE GOING

Though the production is finished, it doesn't mean that the work of the designer is. As with writers, designers need to get people to review their work so it can be improved and validated. Sometimes people only review the things they can write down, but keep in mind that the actual production elements (like the voice recordings and the audio icons) must also be reviewed. Peers can do some of this review work, but a better way to review it is to have the intended audience try it out and see if they like it. And what if they don't? That's the subject of our next chapter.

EIGHT

USABILITY TESTING

You don't hear things that are bad about your company unless you ask. It is easy to hear good tidings, but you have to scratch to get the bad news.
—THOMAS J. WATSON, SR., IBM EXECUTIVE

It's strange—not to mention exasperating—to think that a company would go so far as to conceive, design, and manufacture a product without ever ensuring that people can use it, and just as important, that they like using it. But if my personal experience is any indication, it happens with alarming frequency. I can't count the number of times I've used an appliance and thought to myself, "Surely, the people who designed or produced this have never tried to use it."

A case in point: my clock/radio. It looks great. It sounds great. But it has the worst interface imaginable for programming the radio's preset-station buttons. Instead of having users simply hold down a "Set station" button after they've tuned in the preferred station, it requires them to first press an "Enter" button, *then* press one of the buttons used to jump to another station. Enter? Why in the name of human factors would I "enter" something *before* I've selected it? Shouldn't I select—and *then* enter?

This would only be a minor annoyance were it not for the fact that the radio has no backup battery to protect against a power failure. That means every time my home loses power, I have to rediscover how to reset the radio station buttons. If the designers of this device had to use it themselves for a while, they would surely have encountered the same problems and made appropriate changes.

That's why it's essential for speech-recognition system designers to conduct both usability tests and pilot tests before a system is deployed on a large scale. *Essential?* Couldn't we just skip the usability test, do a pilot test, and see what kind of feedback we get? No. You can't assume a system works fine just because no one has complained about it. As Thomas Watson, Sr., pointed out, people are unlikely to tell you bad things unless you ask them first. And even if people *can* use an application, that doesn't necessarily mean that they *want* to use it. Our goal is to create systems that people actually *prefer* to use, and the only way to ensure this preference is through usability testing.

Usability testing is sometimes confused with *quality assurance* (QA), but the two are very different. QA usually measures a product's performance against its specifications. For example, QA on an automobile would ensure that the components function as specified, that the gaps between the doors and the body are within certain tolerances, and so forth. QA testing would not determine whether a vehicle is easy for people to operate, but usability testing would. In a speech application, QA ensures that the appropriate prompts do in fact play at the right times and in the right order. This kind of testing is important, because designers generally shouldn't assume that an application will work to "spec." QA testing can tell us a great deal about a system's functionality. But it can't tell us if the target population for the application can use it—or will like to use it.

THE VALUE OF USABILITY TESTING

Usability testing answers four key questions about an application.

* Can people use it?

* Do they form a correct mental model of the application so they can continue to use it? That is, do the people using the system form images in their heads (about the way to navigate through the system, the commands to use in particular situations, and so on) that matches the way the system actually works?

* Can they extend their mental model so that they're confident to interact with other areas of the system?

* Do they enjoy using it?

Each successive question demands a higher standard of usability. If people can use an application once, they may or may not be able to use it successfully the next time they call. If they can use it successfully on subsequent attempts, then they probably have formed an accurate mental model of how the system works. And if they actually enjoy using the application ... well, then the designer has hit the jackpot.

HOW WE TEST AN APPLICATION

The basic idea of usability testing is to gather together a small group of people (say, 10 to 15) who represent the population that will use the application. We then ask them to perform a series of tasks, derived from the objectives set out in the Requirements Specification. We observe them as they perform these tasks, noting where they have problems and success. We then correct the problems.

Usability testing is an art in itself—and there are many good books available that explain the methods and processes of usability testing,[1] so we won't go into all the details here. However, most of these books focus on testing *graphical* user interfaces for computer applications, not *audio* user interfaces, such as those found in speech-recognition applications—and there are some significant differences between them.

For example, when testing speech systems, we can't have test subjects speak out loud to give their feedback *while* they're using the system, because that could cause the speech recognizer to malfunction. Instead, we need to look for other reactions, such as body language, to determine when they're having problems.

---

1. A great book is *Usability Engineering* by Jakob Nielsen (San Francisco: Morgan Kaufmann Publishers, 1994).

OBJECTIVES OF USABILITY TESTING

When testing an application, we always keep three questions in mind.

* What *should* the test subjects be doing at each point to get their tasks accomplished?

* What *are* the test subjects doing at each point, and if they aren't doing the right (or optimal) things, what *are* they doing?

* What are the similarities and differences between the mental model of the system that the *subject* is forming and the mental model that the *designer* intended?

Finding the answers to these questions can happen at several points in the process of designing a system.

When is the right time to test an application? It depends on the size. We'd probably want to test a subset of the total functionality of a very large application in stages throughout the design and implementation process. For smaller applications, it just makes sense to test when design and implementation is nearly complete.

PREPARING FOR THE TEST

To get the best test results, you need to do a few things ahead of time.

Test the test. Before getting subjects to test an application, always perform a dry run to ensure that the subjects will be able to use it and that the application hasn't changed (for the worse) since the last time you used it.

Create a pre-test questionnaire. A questionnaire helps designers and testers get a better understanding of the test subjects and their interactions with the system. In addition to such personal data as age and education level, the questionnaire should include application-related questions. For example, if we were testing a brokerage application, we might ask, "Currently, how many times a month do you make trades?" This questionnaire

---

Questionnaire

Subject #

Age: ❏ 18–24   ❏ 25–30   ❏ 31–35   ❏ 36–40
             ❏ 41–45   ❏ 46–50   ❏ 51+

Occupation: _____

Experience:

    At work do you use (check all that apply)

        ❏ Voice mail
        ❏ Answering machine
        ❏ Cellular phone
        ❏ Computer
        ❏ The World Wide Web
        ❏ E-mail

Education:

    Last completed degree

        ❏ High school
        ❏ Undergraduate
        ❏ Masters
        ❏ Doctorate
        ❏ Post-Doctorate

Have you made a flight reservation within the past six months?

    ❏ Yes
    ❏ No

If you answered "yes". . .

    How did you make that reservation?

    _____

FIGURE 8.1 A Sample Pre-Test Questionnaire

mainly serves as reference material to help the tester analyze and interpret the subject's test experience. Figure 8.1 is an example of a pre-test questionnaire that might be used when testing a flight reservation system.

Develop a list of tasks to test. Designers and testers need to decide which tasks the test subjects will be asked to perform during the test. When testing a home banking application, tasks would probably include checking balances and transferring funds. This set of top-tier tasks should be derived from the Requirements Specification. The tasks need to be representative of the most common tasks that users will perform, as well as some of the critical but less used features of the application. Ideally, the entire application would be tested, but sometimes this isn't possible, usually due to time constraints. Most often, the tester chooses a set of three to five tasks from those most commonly used in the system. For a home banking application, the test subjects' tasks might be to check their balances, transfer funds between accounts, and determine if a particular check has been cashed.

Some common tasks can be omitted from the test because they're similar to other tasks being tested. For example, in a brokerage application, there'd be little reason to ask the subject to check a stock's price/earnings ratio if they've already demonstrated their ability to check other information, such as the stock's 52-week high price.

Testers are also unlikely to include tasks that only a small fraction of the target population would ever perform—unless the task is very different in style from the rest of the application or uses some unusual terminology or may be critical for that small population. In those cases, testing would be warranted. If, however, the task is quite standard and the designer and tester agree that it has no esoteric content or style, then usually it won't need to be tested.

Organize a logging method. There are several ways to record the test subject's testing experience—usually videotape, audio tapes of the phone line, and perhaps a **tick-sheet** that the tester will use to note how many times particular events occur. Making a videotape of the test is best because it can be reviewed and reanalyzed later if new issues present themselves. Once the recording method has been established, the testing environment needs to be prepared.

Create a post-test questionnaire. This questionnaire is given to test subjects after they've completed the test. It enables testers and designers to get the test subjects' written answers to questions such as "How well did you like the voice of the system? Rate this on a scale of 1 (not at all) to 5 (very much)" or "List three things that could be changed to improve this system."

Figure 8.2 shows what a sample post-test questionnaire might look like.

When all these preparations are complete, it's time to test. Only one question remains: How do we get the right test subjects?

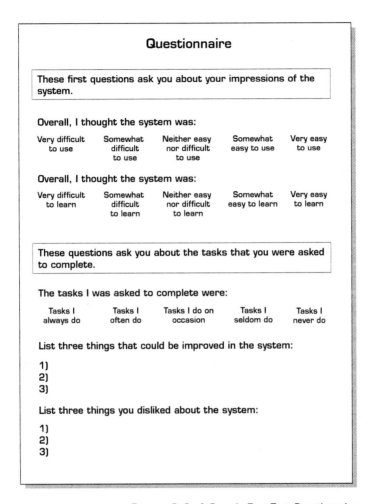

Questionnaire

These first questions ask you about your impressions of the system.

Overall, I thought the system was:

| Very difficult to use | Somewhat difficult to use | Neither easy nor difficult to use | Somewhat easy to use | Very easy to use |

Overall, I thought the system was:

| Very difficult to learn | Somewhat difficult to learn | Neither easy nor difficult to learn | Somewhat easy to learn | Very easy to learn |

These questions ask you about the tasks that you were asked to complete.

The tasks I was asked to complete were:

| Tasks I always do | Tasks I often do | Tasks I do on occasion | Tasks I seldom do | Tasks I never do |

List three things that could be improved in the system:

1)
2)
3)

List three things you disliked about the system:

1)
2)
3)

FIGURE 8.2 A Sample Post-Test Questionnaire

THE TEST SUBJECTS

The results of a usability test are only meaningful if the test subjects are representative of the people who will actually use the application. This may seem obvious, but I've often seen companies use their own employees as test subjects. Sometimes they can give good feedback, particularly if they are the employees who regularly work closely with customers, such as bank tellers or customer service representatives, or when the company is testing an application to be used *by* the company's employees.

However, more often than not, employees want the system to work in a way that works best for them—not for the actual users! For example, if an airline application said, "Please say your reservation code," an airline employee might say, "Well, it should say 'PNR'—for Passenger Name Record. That's what it's called." However, most people who fly don't know what a "PNR" is (though they do understand the concept of a "reservation code"). Employees may be the lowest-cost and most easily available test subjects, but they're clearly not the optimal choice, unless of course the application is intended for employees.

So what kind of people *do* we want to test an application? We want a group of subjects who approximate the intended user population—the closer, the better. For example, let's say we are testing a trading application designed for brokers in the southern U.S. and our test subjects are consumers from northern California who sometimes make trades. The results would not be reliable.

Instead, our test subjects not only should be stockbrokers from the southern U.S., but also should match the gender, age profile, net worth, and brokerage experience of our target population. So if 20% of brokers in the Deep South are under age 30, 60% are under 40, and the rest are under 50, then we'd want to make sure that our test subjects match that age breakdown. The same holds true for the male/female ratio. It makes no sense, for example, to have men testing an application that will be used almost exclusively by women.

HOW TO GET TEST SUBJECTS

It's not always easy to identify test subjects, but here are some effective ways to find the right people. One way is for the tester to ask the client for a random set of potential users. This is useful when the intended user population is highly specialized and it would be difficult (if not impossible) to get the right subjects any other way. So, if we were testing an application for airline flight attendants, we could simply ask the airline about the demographics of the flight attendant population, and then select a sample from it.

Another way to get subjects is to use a professional recruiter. Usually these people recruit for focus groups, but they can be asked to recruit for what would be considered one-on-one interviews. The advantage of using good recruiters is that they can screen the general population by almost any criteria. That is, you could ask for something as crazy and specific as "15 people, 5 who are women, 10 who are men, and all of whom owned a Porsche 911 before 1995 and a Ferrari before 1988. They must all be able to fly small planes, and at least two of them must own and regularly use roller skates. Oh yeah, and the age range should be evenly distributed between 46 and 87." Believe it or not, good recruiters can find these people. And when it's time for the test, good recruiters will call the subjects three times beforehand to confirm each appointment.

The only disadvantage to using recruiters is (you guessed it) that you have to pay them for every subject they find. You also have to pay the subjects an incentive fee, which generally increases according to the subjects' income levels. That means you can probably get college kids to participate in exchange for gift certificates to a local pizza shop, but investment brokers may require the equivalent of two to three hours salary.

THE TEST ENVIRONMENT

Most of the time usability tests are conducted in usability test laboratories. But for some applications, the environment in which the test takes place can affect its outcome. Consider an application that will be used primarily in a noisy, outdoor location. In this example, the indoor laboratory environment might not produce accurate results. In such cases, it makes sense to test in the actual environment in which the application will be used. This may produce some logistical challenges, but the results will be worth it.

TYPES OF TESTS

Typically there is one person who oversees (or in some cases does) all the usability testing. This person's sole role is to evaluate the quality of the design as it works for people. The usability tester doesn't have to be the designer (even though it often works out that way); he or she just needs an intimate knowledge of how the system works and familiarity with how to run a usability test. There are two popular ways to test a speech-recognition application: the **Wizard of Oz** approach and the **classical** approach.

Wizard of Oz Usability Testing

Named for the classic film's "man behind the curtain" who had no real power or wizardry, Wizard of Oz[2] testing is performed without a real system—only a real design.

Simply put, one person pretends to be the computer, while another person acts as the caller. The caller picks up a phone and calls the other person (who is pretending to be the computer). The computer person can *either* speak the prompts just as the computer would—"I'm sorry, I didn't understand you. Please say 'Red,' 'Green,' or 'Blue'"—or use a slightly more sophisticated variation of the Wizard of Oz test involving some technology. This version would involve having the computer person control and play a set of audio files in response to the caller at the other end of the phone. This method sounds more like a real system (because actual audio prompts are used), but it requires additional time to record the files and set up the test and a method to allow a person to quickly choose the right audio prompt to play.

Classical Usability Testing

The classical approach calls for the designer to recruit the services of a usability-testing laboratory. Each caller/test subject is placed inside a room with a phone, a chair, a desk—and a video camera to capture audio and facial expressions. In this method, the test subject calls into a real speech-recognition system. The sounds on the phone line (as well as the ambient room sounds) are also recorded.

---

2. The term "Wizard of Oz" as applied to usability testing comes from J. F. Kelly, and can be found in his unpublished doctoral dissertation, "Natural Language and Computers: Six empirical steps for writing an easy-to-use computer application," The Johns Hopkins University, 1983. (It can be obtained from University Microfilms International, 300 North Zeeb Road, Ann Arbor, MI 48106.)

Wizard of Oz versus Classical Usability Testing

Which method of testing is better? Well, they both use the right population. And both of them ask callers to perform real tasks that mimic the system in real life. But the classical method will give the designer/tester more insight. Because it uses a real system, the classical usability test also enables the designer to test the quality of the recognition engine and whether it understands the caller's responses correctly. This can't happen in a Wizard of Oz test, where a real person pretends to be the computer.

The Wizard of Oz approach is a double-edged sword since it enables the tester to ignore system performance—beneficial when the system hasn't been built yet, but detrimental if performance issues aren't discovered before deployment. If test subjects are using a real system, they will encounter the problems associated with using a real system, such as delays while the database is looking something up. In a real system, a caller might have to wait up to 30 seconds for the database to come back with an answer. (In that case, the designer might want to prepare users to wait for a while, so they don't think the system is broken. But with the Wizard of Oz approach, the person who is pretending to be the computer might simply say, "Please hold while I get that information," then quickly come back and say the next line, "OK, I've got your checking account information"—not knowing that the real (and yet to be built) system may have long or unpredictable database delays.

No matter which testing method you use, you will gain insight into whether people understand the prompts, know what to say, and get their tasks accomplished.

THE TEST IS OVER—NOW WHAT?

After the test, the results need to be tabulated and grouped by the tester. Often testers describe the problems and then rank them on two scales. One scale rates the severity of the problem: Is it a showstopper or just a minor annoyance? The second scale ranks the problem by the level of difficulty required to correct it; does it entail major database and application recoding—or just a minor change to the prompt wording?

Here's a typical example of how a usability issue would be reported.

Severity = High

Change = Minor

Problem = Prompt 10072 says "If you're done, say 'Main menu'" when it should say "If you're done, say 'Good-bye.'" Six of ten users didn't know how to end the call.

The tester and the rest of the team determine which problems to fix after they have been ranked. Once major changes have been made, it's often time for another usability test. If the changes are all minor, it's time to go on to pilot testing.

INTERPRETING TEST RESULTS

Many parts of the usability test require the tester to fathom what's going on in test subjects' heads when they're not saying anything—and that can be a tricky business. I've seen people who struggled with an application and, when presented with three choices, said the two "wrong" choices several times. When I first witnessed this, I was amazingly frustrated and wanted to blurt out "Just say the other choice!" But professionalism prevailed and eventually they said the right choice (after a LONG while).

At the time I thought that either the test subjects must be stupid, or I was totally unclear when I explained the task. Actually, I was wrong on both counts. What had happened was that the subjects had heard part of an introduction prompt that caused them to form a different mental model than the one the designer had in mind. The test subjects tried to adhere to this mental model until finally giving up and trying the "correct" command. It was at this point that they began to form the correct mental model—but clearly in a less than optimal way. When I realized what had happened, I suggested that the designer change the introductory message—and the problem went away.

On another occasion, I saw a test subject struggle with an application—only to later write on the post-test questionnaire that she loved it! I was flabbergasted! The explanation? The test subject hadn't remembered struggling with the system, because she eventually got her tasks accomplished. But she did remember—and appreciated—the way the system helped her when she was "stuck." This example teaches us an invaluable lesson: The perceived quality of a system isn't always related to the subjects' ability to fly through it without problems—but rather, how well it helps users when they experience a problem.

As these experiences suggest, usability tests are vital—but they are only one step in the process from development to deployment. That's why we continue to observe and change the application during the pilot test.

WHERE WE'VE BEEN—WHERE WE'RE GOING

Understanding the problems that people have with a system and then being able to correct these problems is the only way to make a speech-recognition application that people can use and want to use. Being able to examine the application in a controlled laboratory environment is a good start, but there is no comparison to seeing how it performs in the real world, by motivated callers who need to use that system.

NINE

DEPLOYMENT

Genius begins great works; labor alone finishes them.

—JOSEPH JOUBERT, FRENCH ESSAYIST

Our success derives from sustained intensity.

—ANONYMOUS

The successful conclusion of usability testing—and the completion of any redesigns necessitated by it—are important milestones in the speech-recognition production life-cycle, but by no means indicate that your work is finished.

Sometimes when clients have all their phone lines set up and their system ready to take phone calls, they ask, "Why can't I just turn it on? I did that with my touchtone system." It's an understandable question; after all, many technologies do come ready to work, right out of the box. But speech-recognition systems do not always work perfectly from Day One. Why not? Because verifying the successful operation of the intricacies of a speech-recognition is much more difficult than verifying a touchtone system.

When people are asked to respond to a touchtone system, they do so by pressing one or more of the 12 buttons on a telephone keypad. So, for example, if it's a system that provides movie show times, it's very easy to verify that when callers press "1" for the first movie, the correct information is played. It's also easy to verify that the system is properly rejecting incorrect responses when callers press invalid buttons. (These rejections usually come in the form of a rude, often untrue, and painfully time-consuming prompt, such as "That input was not valid. Please listen to the options and select one of the choices.") As a result, by the time a touchtone system is deployed, the people who designed and tested it should be highly confident that it works.

Not so with a speech-recognition system. When testing a speech-recognition system in a laboratory environment, it's hard to replicate "real world" conditions. And since there is often no single acceptable answer to a prompt, we can't even be sure that callers will say the right things in the first place. Yes, usability testing gives some insight into these issues, but there is simply no substitute for real data from real callers making real calls under real world conditions.

For example, how many ways do you think people might say a four-digit number like "1687?" If it's the part number of a product you're ordering, you might say "one, six, eight, seven." If it's a flight number, you might say "sixteen eighty-seven." And if it's the amount of a cash transfer, you might say "one thousand six hundred eighty-seven." But we can't be sure that *everyone else* calling in to a speech-recognition system will say those numbers the same way. When speech scientists tune the vocabulary of a system, they need to know what actual people are actually saying. They need to listen to thousands of utterances of people saying these numbers, build statistical models to analyze the responses, and then make any necessary changes to improve the recognition.

In many ways, deploying a speech-recognition application is like deploying any other computer software application. No software company simply tests its code internally and then ships it out the door to the customers. Instead, they often deploy it in at least two phases (alpha and beta) to small numbers of select customers. These customers agree to try the software and report any problems or bugs. This process enables the software company to see how its code works in the real world—and to remedy any problems that arise—before releasing it on a large scale. This is similar to the process used in deploying a speech-recognition application.

But there's an important difference between commercial software and speech-recognition systems. When commercial, shrink-wrapped software is deployed, customers have a way to report bugs to the company so that it can still make changes to future versions. Speech-recognition systems don't allow the user to easily do this since the software doesn't reside in the hands of the caller. And callers don't have a manual to tell them what to do if they find problems or who to contact with technical support questions. And due to the size of most speech applications, testing with a relatively small number of subjects won't uncover all the potential problems. For this reason, it's critical that companies deploy speech-recognition applications in a deliberate, phased approach.

A similar approach is used in Hollywood, where movie studios almost always conduct advance screenings of films for "real" audiences to gauge their reactions and, if necessary, make changes. These changes may occur before the movie is put into general release, but also after the movie has been released to particular markets. Sometimes these changes are major. For example, director Frank Capra shot and tested four different endings to his 1941 film classic, *Meet John Doe*, starring Gary Cooper and Barbara Stanwyck. In one, Cooper's character commits suicide. In another, Stanwyck's character persuades him not to leap from the top of City Hall. Unsatisfied with the response to these and two other endings, Capra filmed a fifth (and the final) ending, in which Stanwyck talks some sense into Cooper and then faints into his arms.

A determined artist may not care what the public thinks about a work of art—in fact, some even view widespread popularity as a sign of artistic failure—but as with film, speech-recognition designers don't have that choice. To be considered a success, their work has to be understood and widely used and enjoyed by their intended audience. And the only sure way to achieve these objectives is through a careful, controlled, and monitored multi-phase deployment.

THE IMPORTANCE OF MULTI-PHASE DEPLOYMENT

Before we discuss the benefits of deploying in multiple phases, let's examine the pitfalls of *not* deploying in phases.

Let's say we're operating a large call center. In anticipation of launching our new speech-recognition system, we've rerouted our phone lines, and trained and reassigned thousands of agents to handle other tasks. The big day comes, we throw the metaphorical switch, and—*ta-dah!*—our system is fully deployed.

But there's a problem. Perhaps the system can't handle the call volume for technical reasons. Or maybe we start getting hundreds of calls from frustrated or angry callers who were given the wrong information by the system or who stumble over a particular question (that was never encountered by usability testers) almost every time. We'd probably have to shut the system down to fix these problems. That means our agents would have to return to their old responsibilities—at least temporarily. Our phone lines might have to be reconfigured. And in all the pandemonium and confusion, we might be completely offline and unavailable for hours. Imagine the cost—in dollars, in customer dissatisfaction, in employee disgruntlement, and potentially, in bad press. It's simply not worth it.

The insights and peace of mind we gain by deploying a system in phases greatly outweighs any expense in resources or time associated with it. In fact, to have a successful transition to a speech-recognition system from a touchtone system or from live agents, a planned deployment is a requirement.

THE THREE PHASES OF DEPLOYMENT

Speech-recognition systems should be deployed in three progressive phases.

1. In the pilot deployment phase, only a few hundred calls are allowed into the system. The designers and programmers then tune up everything as needed—the recognizer, the design of the user interface, any technical glitches, and perhaps even the prompts. The relatively low volume of calls can be analyzed manually. It's a little time-consuming, but easy to do and yields great payback.

2. Only move on to the partial deployment phase once you're certain that all known issues have been worked out and the system is running smoothly. The system takes more calls—perhaps as many as 10,000—to get a larger sample of data over a longer period of time. Because of the larger volume, most of the calls are analyzed using automated methods, but you should still do some manual analysis of problem calls.

3. In the full deployment phase, the call volume is increased to the system's full capacity while the designers and programmers continue to monitor the system, albeit at longer intervals than before, using almost entirely automated means.

PILOT DEPLOYMENT

Pilot deployment is usually the longest phase of the deployment process; almost all of the data analysis work must be performed manually, and more changes need to be made than in later phases.

Here's how it works. We listen to the first 100 calls from 100 *different* people. We don't want to analyze repeat callers (the data wouldn't be valid if it were, say, 20 calls from only 5 different people). We then listen to see how these 100 people use the system and determine if the system is doing the right things at the right times.

We have two primary concerns in this phase: **accuracy** and **transaction completion**. We measure accuracy by monitoring the recognizer's ability to correctly identify what callers said. We measure transaction completion by tracking how many callers were successful in completing their tasks.

For example, let's say we're in pilot deployment for a telephone banking system. A user calls in to the system, identifies herself, and says, "Transfer funds." The system recognizes the command and prompts the caller for the two accounts involved, but can't understand when the caller says how much money to transfer. It sends her back to the main menu or to a "live" operator for help.

Assuming that the caller says a valid amount and calls from an acoustical environment where we would expect the recognizer to work (rather than, say, the baggage claim area of an airport), this call would be considered a failure in both recognition and transaction completion. However, if the caller eventually learned to enter the amount using touchtones—and she did indeed accomplish her task—we would consider the call a success in transaction completion but a failure in recognition.

Our goal, of course, is to have a system that is highly accurate and that has a high rate of transaction completion. But we don't necessarily weigh these two measurements equally. Ultimately, as shown in the example above, transaction completion is the more important metric, because enabling callers to accomplish their tasks is more important than understanding everything they say. After all, some callers may have heavy accents or may be calling from noisy locations. Conversely, a high accuracy rate and a low transaction completion rate would indicate serious design problems, since the low transaction completion number could not be attributable to recognition problems.

What do we consider "acceptable" rates of accuracy and transaction completion? While there are no hard and fast rules—and all systems are different—the recognition should be good enough that callers can get through their calls without getting frustrated. The overall transaction completion rate should be between 80 to 85% before moving on to partial deployment. Of course, the most desirable outcome is both a high accuracy rate and a high transaction completion rate.

Identifying Pilot Testers

The first and most important step in pilot deployment is to find the right population to use the system. Just as in usability testing, it's important to find people who are representative of the calling population to ensure that the results will be accurate. This process won't be the same as in usability testing, where we might have used a professional recruiter. It is essential to get real callers who need to use the system. That means designers and their clients should not send a company-wide e-mail to employees telling them to "call in to the following number to try out our new speech-activated customer service system." We don't want any ringers. (Proud family members of the designer are also disqualified.) However, it may be a good idea to alert the customer service representatives that there is a new system in place so they will know what customers are talking about and can take notes when customers complain about or compliment the new system.

Depending on the system, there are a variety of ways to get the right people to call in. For example, if we were creating a flight information system to replace an existing touchtone system, we could simply take one-tenth of 1% of all calls and route them to the new system. If, however, we were testing a credit card information system, we might send out newsletters to several hundred randomly selected customers asking them to update their records and call a new number for account information. This isn't a perfect strategy, because some people may not call the new number or even read the mail sent to them by the bank (I know I don't read anything included in my credit card statement except how much I owe).

Another approach is to select calls as they come in, using caller ID information to aid in segmenting the population of callers. This method enables us to roll out a system geographically—for example, testing only callers in different area codes before rolling it out nationwide. This strategy is especially useful when we know the demographic attributes within each area code, such as the urban/rural mix, ethnic composition, education levels, and income levels. We can then test using a set of diverse callers.

Whichever method is chosen, clients should avoid testing the system during times that are not representative of the entire year. That means an airline shouldn't turn on a new system the day before Thanksgiving, nor if at all possible should an online brokerage firm test its new system when the stock market is especially volatile.

Configuring the System for Testing

Before starting the test, the designer may consider placing a temporary prompt in the system alerting callers that they are about to try a new system. This not only prepares the caller for any "hiccups" in the system, but also prevents them from being surprised if the system isn't available to them the next time they call.

Some companies keep these temporary prompts simple: "Welcome to our new flight information system." Others go to greater lengths to ensure the message is totally clear: "Welcome to our new speech-activated system. Currently it's only available during business hours, and in order to ensure your satisfaction, there may be times when it's being improved and you'll be unable to use it to access your account information." This kind of prompt is useful if the client is trying to expose the system to valuable customers and wants to avoid jeopardizing their satisfaction and loyalty. However, such a long statement will *quickly* get boring, so it's a good idea, if possible, to play it only once for each caller. This can be accomplished through programming. For example, the system can be set up to play the long prompt only the first time any given account number is entered. Callers hear it only once and will more likely be patient with any problems.

Being Prepared to Stop the Test

Being prepared to start the test is essential. So is being prepared to *stop* the test at a moment's notice. When a system is being launched for the first time, almost anything can go wrong. In most cases, the system uses a new type of computer, connected to a new database, using new hardware to connect to the phone lines. There are multiple potential points of failure—and they may have nothing at all to do with the people designing and deploying the system. For example, the phone company may not be sending calls to the system correctly, or perhaps there's a previously undiscovered bug in the computer operating system. Of course, we can't rule out the possibility of a problem with the design, either.

Whatever the cause, if something occurs to compromise, invalidate, or incapacitate the test, we always need a plan and a procedure that will enable us to turn off the system and have all the calls go back to where they used to go. If it's an entirely new system that isn't replacing a prior call center or touchtone system, calls should be routed to a dedicated computer that simply announces that the system is down for service and then hangs up—*gracefully*. Perhaps it should also provide information about how the caller can contact the company via other channels.

Clearly, if something goes awry, we have to be prepared to respond immediately—and that means we have to watch the system like hawks. This is why it makes sense to limit the pilot test to normal business hours. This ensures that someone is there to monitor the system and that any third-party hardware or software vendors can be contacted for customer support in the event of an emergency. (Even companies with 24-hour customer support don't always have the *most* knowledgeable people standing by in the middle of the night.)

Once the test is running and people are monitoring its operation, you can start to examine and analyze the calls coming into the system.

Analyzing and Categorizing Calls

The system logs calls as they come in and stores the data—including actual audio files of calls—in a database. In addition to some manual analyses, we also analyze calls using a software tool that provides a graphical view of the logged data.

The capabilities and functions of analysis tools vary by vendor, but the best ones enable the team to view statistics such as the average call duration and the average number of transactions. They pinpoint problem areas by providing a view into individual states where the recognizer is having problems. The best tools *also* allow us to listen to each utterance of any call so we can gain a clearer understanding of what happened in that call—and whether or not the system is working for the callers.

We examine the calls from the callers' perspective to determine the objectives of their calls and their impressions about the system. Based on all the data we collect and analyze, we put each call into one of the three categories: success, failure, or unknown.

Successes

If we hear a caller effortlessly getting information and accomplishing her tasks promptly, we can consider that call a success—particularly if she sounds nonchalant and closes the conversation with a friendly sign-off, such as "Good-bye."

But it's harder to determine the success of some other calls. For example, when working with United Airlines to deploy a system to handle employee travel reservations, we received several puzzling calls. Employees would call in, search for flights, and get right to the point where they could make a reservation—and then they would hang up. Were they successes? What defines a success? The callers didn't complete the expected transaction or say "Good-bye"—but they didn't sound upset, either. So what was happening?

After more research we found out that many employees were calling to see how many available seats there were on the flights they wanted. Often, if there was limited space, they wouldn't make the reservation. We discovered that this was related to how the airline determines who can fly for free. Employees with the most seniority or higher-level jobs can get on flights with only one available seat just by checking in at the gate. Employees who were hired more recently are considered lower-priority fliers and as such, are more likely to get bumped off a crowded flight. That was why they would call, check seating availability, and then hang up. Since they were successful in getting the information they wanted—even though they didn't make reservations—we categorized these calls as successes.

It's not always possible to know what all the success criteria will be before deploying the application, so it is critical to examine the calls later on to see if you overlooked some success criteria. During the testing process, it's important to look for unusual patterns such as this to ensure accurate test results.

Failures

Some failures are obvious. For example, if we listen to a call and hear someone not being recognized, yelling at the system, and using profanity, that's a definite failure. Sometimes a failure occurs when the system simply does one thing wrong—for example, correctly understanding that a caller wants to talk to "Zach Westelman" and transferring the call correctly to Zach Westelman, but incorrectly telling the caller that he's being transferred to "Ben McCormack." This is still considered a failure, because if the problem were left uncorrected, it would inevitably result in lots of hang-ups and confused or frustrated callers.

There are only three, mutually exclusive categories of calls—success, failure, and unknown. So, what if a call starts off and proceeds successfully, but ends as a failure? Since we have no "semi-success" category and our goal is to improve the system (not whitewash the results), I'd recommend treating such calls as failures.

Unknowns

We call the third category of calls "unknowns." Sometimes after reviewing the data we collect—and even listening to the audio files—we are simply unable to determine whether a call was successful or not. For example, sometimes a call starts and then there is an immediate hang-up. Or perhaps a caller uses the system successfully for a while, and then abruptly hangs up for no apparent reason.

There are many explanations for why this happens, and it's often no fault of the system or its design. If a hang-up is the first and only sound on the call, it could be a wrong number. If a caller is using the system without problems and then abruptly hangs up, it could mean that they were interrupted or they had a bad mobile phone connection. Calls are considered failures in cases where callers' behavior doesn't tell us enough about their intent to categorize it.

There are bound to be a few unknown calls during any test, and if the percentage is small, there's no need for further investigation. However—as we learned in the United Airlines example above—if unknown calls represent a significant percentage of all calls, it's definitely worth checking out.

Fixing the Right Problems

The whole idea of listening to test calls is to identify and understand any patterns that emerge in the system and as it is used. By actually hearing the calls, a development team can quickly understand what callers are experiencing. By reviewing the data and running statistics on them, the team can spot trends and act quickly to fix the "right problems," rather than risk a misdiagnosis and fix something that's actually working well. To paraphrase a surgeon I once heard, we don't want to take out the appendix when it's the tonsils that are causing the problem.

Sometimes, major problems emerge in testing—problems that necessitate an equally major redesign of all or some of the system. However, having a large number of failed calls in a pilot test doesn't necessarily dictate a wholesale redesign. For example, if we find that 80 out of 100 calls are failing, but we understand the problem behind 76 of them—and we know how to correct it—we can move ahead knowing we have only four calls that need further investigation.

Let's say we designed a system for an entertainment ticket sales company. It includes a prompt that says, "You can say 'Movies,' 'Music,' 'Theater,' or 'Talk to an operator.'" What if, during the pilot test, we found that 58% of the callers asked to talk to an operator? We couldn't automatically assume that the system was a failure. People may have been opting to talk to an operator because they needed help with something the system wasn't designed to handle. In that case, it may be OK to leave the system as is—or, if it made sense, we might consider adding functionality to the system to reduce the volume of calls going to call center representatives. But if further investigation revealed that callers simply didn't know that the system could handle their requests, we would definitely want to modify the design to ensure that callers know what the system can and cannot do.

"What We've Got Here Is Failure to Communicate"[1]

It's often important to look beyond the speech-recognition system for the source of problems when they crop up. Take the United Airlines Bag Desk application, for example. The system had been up and running successfully for several months when, all of a sudden, a significant number of calls were being categorized as failures by the automated analysis tools. When the people on the team analyzed the problem calls, they discovered that all of the callers were saying they had lost their bags in "Jackson, Mississippi."

---

1. Spoken by Captain, Road Prison 36 in the movie *Cool Hand Luke* (1967).

It turned out that "Jackson, Mississippi" wasn't in the recognition vocabulary because, as far as the team knew, United didn't fly in or out of the Jackson airport. So, the system had worked properly, correctly rejecting what people were saying and transferring them to United agents. But the question remained: Why were people calling United to report lost baggage at an airport without United service?

The development team called the United technical team. Neither group could figure it out—until a few calls were made to United officials. It turned out that United had just recently inaugurated service at the Jackson airport, but not all of the airline's databases had yet been updated, and the people in charge of the system hadn't been informed. Once the source of the problem was identified, the team was able to update the system in a matter of hours and its failure rate dropped once again.

A sudden jump in the failure rate is not the only way to spot a problem in a deployed system. A good analysis tool will monitor the system and—if anything out of the normal range occurs—send an alarm by either pager or e-mail to the people in charge of system administration.

Knowing When to End Pilot Deployment

Every development team has to establish a grading system to signal when it's appropriate to end the pilot deployment phase and move on to partial deployment. The following are some rules of thumb.

* *If fewer than 5% of calls are failures*, the system is ready for partial deployment.

* *If between 5% and 20% of calls are failures*, we need to figure out what we can do to fix the application promptly.

* *If more than 20% of calls are failures*, we should seriously consider turning off the application until problems are identified and solved.

* *If more than 33% of calls are categorized as unknown*, we need to gather more data to help us analyze the application.

Making Changes

Once the calls have been categorized, the problem calls should be divided into subcategories. This helps the development team pinpoint the areas of the application causing problems for callers. Once they identify the sources of any problems, the development team proposes potential fixes, making sure to consider what effect, if any, the fix will have on the recognizer and the usability of the rest of the application.

Once the appropriate changes have been made, we turn the system on again to collect another set of calls. If the failure rate drops to 5% or lower, it's time to turn up the volume through partial deployment.

PARTIAL DEPLOYMENT

In partial deployment, our line of questioning shifts from "Does the system work?" (because we know it does) to "How can we improve it?" Partial deployment is basically the same thing as pilot deployment—only this time the system takes more calls over a longer period of time. How much time? It varies, depending on the client and the application. Some applications are so complex that they need to be rolled out very slowly over a period of months, while others may be so small and simple that they can be fully deployed in a matter of days. Because we're talking about a much larger volume of calls, more of the analysis will be performed by software tools and less by listening to individual calls.

Unlike pilot deployment, where we focus on tuning up all the severe problems, partial deployment focuses more on trends such as periodic equipment failure (a bad hard drive?) or subtle shifts in callers' usage patterns. Because partial deployment is closer to *real life usage*, we're able to monitor system performance under a wider range of conditions, including times of high call volume. We can see, for example, how promptly and efficiently calls are handled when the computing power and phone lines are reaching their limits. If things are going well at this point, we may be tempted to simply open the floodgates and go straight to full deployment—but that's a temptation generally to be avoided.

We don't want our entire calling population to become totally dependent on a system that may not be quite ready for all of the people, all of the time.

For example, perhaps we could make the calls go faster by cutting out any unnecessary silence (dead air) in the prompts. A few seconds of dead air may not seem like much, but after ten million calls they can add up to some hefty—and totally unnecessary—long distance charges. Some subtle improvements in deployed systems have been known to contribute to a savings of one million dollars a year—accomplished simply by editing some of the prompts!

We also keep our eyes open for more subtle trends, such as trying to see if callers are exhibiting repeated behaviors that we can capitalize on for improvement, speed, and elegance. So, for example, if most callers who call in to a credit card company ask for a particular piece of information every time they call (like their credit card balance), the design could monitor the callers' performance and change its behavior to satisfy these callers. Instead of forcing them to ask for that information every time they call, the system could *automatically* offer to play that information at the beginning of every call.

When we go from pilot to partial deployment, we go from analyzing hundreds of calls to analyzing thousands of calls. The added volume can often reveal failures that didn't appear in the pilot phase. Why? Because the more calls we get, the greater the chance that groups of people will say something the system doesn't recognize.

The United Airlines Baggage Desk is an example of an application where the only way to improve it was by analyzing lots of calls. In order for the system to provide status information for a lost bag, it asked the caller, "Where did you file your claim?" In partial deployment, we discovered that, although most callers gave an expected response (for example, "Chicago O'Hare" or "L-A-X"), a small percentage of callers replied in a completely logical, valid, but unfortunately unanticipated way, saying "At the airport."

We saw two solutions to the problem.

1. We could change the question to **"At which airport did you file the claim?"**

2. We could program the system to respond differently when a caller said, **"At the airport"** by following up with another question: **"What's the name of the airport?"**

Both solutions would probably work. So which one did we select?

We ended up choosing the first option, and here's why. While sometimes changing the wording of an existing prompt may cause confusion among current users, it's worth doing if the system is relatively new. Also, changing how this program worked (adding another turn to the dialogue) would necessitate more development work and quality assurance testing, which could delay the launch of the system. And in this case, changing the call flow wasn't the best solution, especially since modifying just one prompt was all that was really necessary.

FULL DEPLOYMENT

The transition from partial to full deployment can and should be a seamless process. When the system is stable and working well for callers, we can keep adding to the call volume until it's taking 100% of the calls 24 hours a day, 7 days a week, all year long. At this point we're considered to be in full deployment.

By the time we reach full deployment, we've generally tapered off the monitoring frequency to about once a month. After a few months, we can monitor even less frequently (only having someone listen to about 100 calls every 4 months). At this stage, almost all analysis is performed using statistics and automated processes. Whatever improvements we make to the system now should be minor and subtle.

Above all, we have to make sure that we're using the same metrics we used in partial deployment. The more information we have to analyze the system, the more accurate the results. If we only analyzed the calls on a single day, we might see transaction completion percentages as high as 96% or 94%. But, just as baseball players' batting averages often drop from April to July as they get more at-bats, transaction completion numbers, averaged over a long period of time, could show a drop to an average of 88%, for example. Once again, this helps the development team get a better understanding of how well the system is actually performing.

Even after a system has been deployed, it's essential to continue monitoring its accuracy and transaction completion rates. Often, changes in these numbers can help identify problems. For example, if, after a system has been up and running for six months, its transaction completion rate suddenly dropped from 98% to 86%, we would know there was a problem—especially if the recognition accuracy rate remained high.

Here's why it can happen. Let's say a bank starts calling a particular checking account the "Active Account" as part of an advertising campaign. If callers using the system pick up that phrase from the advertisements and start using it—for example, asking the system to transfer funds from their "Active Accounts" instead of their "Checking" or "Savings" accounts—it's likely the system wouldn't have been programmed to recognize the phrase and, thus, would reject it.

Time enables us to see the longitudinal behavior of the system better. We can gain valuable insights that we can use to improve the system in subtle ways. That's why it's important never to consider a system completely finished. It is always a work in progress, a living thing that must adapt to change and circumstances, just as we all do in our lives. Regular, consistent monitoring over time is the only way to ensure that the people who use and depend on the system can continue to use it effectively and enjoy using it. After all, that's why we make these systems in the first place, right?

WHERE WE'VE BEEN—WHERE WE'RE GOING

We've learned a lot about the ideas surrounding the design process—from research, to prompt writing, brand interpretation, usability testing methods, and tactical aspects of the deployment process. However, nothing can reify the concepts better than a detailed examination of real-world case studies.

PART III

APPLIED KNOWLEDGE

The previous chapters have been arranged in the order that a designer would approach solving a problem. By studying the language and the structures used on systems that have been deployed on a large-scale, we gain insight into the manifestation of the design process. This section examines real-world deployments to see how particular problems have been solved, successfully.

Examining, mimicking, and copying other work is a great way to refine your art as a designer—all artists go to museums to copy other artist's work so that they can attempt to understand the underpinnings of how other artists expressed themselves. However, it's necessary to do more than just copy designs that you see in the real world—you need to understand why those elements worked in a particular application. Sometimes designers can copy the exact words from an application but find that it doesn't work in their own— perhaps because it was the direction of the voice talent that conveyed a layer of meaning beyond the text of the prompts, or perhaps it was the placement of the phrase within the larger context of the application.

This section presents examples derived from deployed applications and explanations for each. These examples should illuminate how several design techniques from the proceeding chapters have been embodied in real applications. However, the importance of simultaneously considering both the tactical aspects of design and the philosophical ones cannot be understated. The Postscript is a historical narrative that serves as a paradigm illustrating the type of victory that can be achieved when the connection between tactical design and philosophical intent is met.

TEN

CASE STUDIES

I haven't taught people in 50 years what my father taught by example in
one week.

—MARIO CUOMO, U.S. POLITICIAN AND AUTHOR

This chapter uses examples from real applications to demonstrate how the ideas in this
book are expressed in state-of-the-art designs. These examples give insight into things
that have been done in the past, and should be viewed for the underlying ideas they convey rather than the actual way that any given solution must be embodied in new designs.

While these examples reflect technological capabilities ranging from 1997 to 2002,
please keep in mind that as the technology progresses—and as people become more
familiar with this type of interface—the state of the art in design will also evolve. However,
to achieve good design, and to ensure that these examples have credibility, work was done
far after the usability testing process. The applications that embodied the examples were
monitored and improved upon long after the general public was exposed to them.

UNITED AIRLINES: SHORTCUTS FOR FREQUENT FLIERS

Flight information systems were one of the earliest types of commercial speech-recognition
applications. The United Airlines system has been in operation since 1999 and receives

an average of two million calls per month. Between 1999 and 2002 this system saved United Airlines in excess of $25 million over the touchtone system that previously was in place.[1] While business travelers are an airline's most profitable customers, they are not their sole customers, so it only makes sense that the United Airlines system provides expedited flight information for those callers who know their flight numbers as well as those who don't. Here's how a typical call goes.

SYSTEM: Welcome to United Airlines' flight information system. I'll be able to help you get information on all United, United Express, and United Shuttle flights. Enter or say the flight number, or say "I don't know it" if you're unsure.

CALLER: *Flight 455.*

SYSTEM: Would you like arrival or departure information?

CALLER: *Departure.*

SYSTEM: OK, I'll look up that information. Hold on. <Database look-up.> Flight 455 is scheduled to depart on time at 8:45 A.M. from Boston Logan, Terminal C, Gate 14. You can say "Repeat that" to hear it again, or "Good-bye" if you're done.

CALLER: *Good-bye.*

This system was designed with two calling populations in mind. The primary audience is frequent-flier business travelers. Because these callers use the system frequently—and are always in a hurry—they're interested in learning how to get quick responses to their inquiries. This system teaches them that they'll get the fastest service if they provide the flight number—either by saying it or by entering it on the telephone keypad. After that, all they need to do is specify whether they want arrival or departure information, and the entire call can go very quickly. In fact, callers can make the call even shorter by "barging in"—interrupting the initial prompt by saying or entering the flight number.

The other people who call flight information systems are friends, relatives, and colleagues checking to see when they need to pick up their parties at the airport. Often these

---

1. Bob Bongiorno, Managing Director of Customer Service, Planning and Finance Applications, United Airlines, at SpeechWorks International Global Speech Day "Web Seminar," May 22, 2002.

people are unaware of the flight numbers, and may not even know the exact time of the scheduled arrival. So, a very different type of experience is needed for these callers—hence, the use of the "I don't know it" command.

The "I don't know it" command mimics the interaction a person might have with another person. We could use another prompt, such as "Enter or say the flight number or say 'Find the flight number' if you don't have it," but that would be cumbersome and unnatural in this context—particularly considering that millions of people of all ages call into the system.

Also note the use of the word "it" in the command—"I don't know *it*." There's a reason why "it" is there. Although some people might use an abbreviated command, such as "I don't know," that doesn't make sense grammatically, because it doesn't specify exactly what the caller doesn't know. Try saying these two examples out loud and compare the way they sound.

> SYSTEM: **Say the flight number or say "I don't know it."**
> CALLER: *I don't know it.*

Or:

> SYSTEM: **Say the flight number or say "I don't know."**
> CALLER: *I don't know.*

The second one just doesn't sound right. And would anyone think that they're reducing the time of the call by omitting the word "it?" In fact, recognizers are more accurate when the utterances are longer than shorter. And while the "it" sound in *this* example won't improve recognition accuracy because it doesn't change the overall sound of the utterance considerably or add much to the length, in certain contexts small additions can make a significant difference.

UNITED AIRLINES: PROVIDING EXTRA
HELP FOR THOSE WHO NEED IT

Now, let's look at what happens when someone calling United Airlines doesn't know the flight number.

SYSTEM: Welcome to United Airlines' flight information system. I'll be able to help you get information on all United, United Express, and United Shuttle flights. Enter or say the flight number or say "I don't know it" if you're unsure.

CALLER: *Uh, I don't know it?*

SYSTEM: OK, we'll find it a different way. Oh, here's a hint: If you ever know the answer to a question I'm asking, you can always interrupt me, and if you get stuck, say "Help." Here goes: Would you like arrival or departure information?

CALLER: *Departure.*

SYSTEM: OK, and from which city is the flight departing?

CALLER: *Boston.*

SYSTEM: ... and in which city does the flight arrive?

CALLER: *Los Angeles.*

SYSTEM: United serves more than one airport in the Los Angeles area. They are: Los Angeles International Airport, Santa Anna—

CALLER: *(Caller barges in and cuts off the playing of the prompt) Los Angeles International.*

SYSTEM: OK, and about what time is the flight scheduled to depart?

CALLER: *8:30?*

SYSTEM: In the morning or in the evening?

CALLER: *Morning.*

SYSTEM: OK, I'll look for flights that have that itinerary, hold on. <Database look-up> I found a few flights that match that itinerary—three, to be exact. Help me find the right flight. Here's the first one on my list: Option 1, Flight 487, departs Boston at 9:15 A.M. and arrives at Los Angeles International at 12:55 P.M. You can say "This one" or "Next" to move on.

CALLER: *This one.*

SYSTEM: **OK, hold on while I get the flight information for Flight 487. <Database look-up> Flight 487 is delayed and will be departing Boston at 9:55 A.M.**

Clearly, it's a longer process when the caller doesn't know the flight number—and people who use the system frequently quickly learn to have the flight numbers before they call. But it's also important to make sure that the millions of infrequent callers don't feel bad because they don't know the number. That's why we use the phrase "That's OK, we'll find it a different way." It's designed to relax callers, letting them know that the system doesn't really care which method they use. At the same time, it subtly reminds callers that they can get their information even faster the next time if they know the flight numbers.

Also note that it is only at the beginning of collecting the itinerary that the system tells callers they can barge in to interrupt the prompt, and say "Help" for more information. Why? There are two reasons. First, it would be a lengthy and cumbersome message to play to each and every caller every time they used the system. Second, callers who call into the system multiple times will quickly know to barge in and interrupt a familiar prompt, so they don't need to be constantly retaught. The "Help" command needs to be there to alert all callers what to do if there are any problems—for example, if the system doesn't understand them or doesn't hear something they say.

Perhaps the most interesting part of the second example is the following phrase.

"I found a few flights that match that itinerary—three, to be exact. Help me find the right flight. Here's the first one on my list."

Now, we could have had the system simply say, "Three flights almost matched your itinerary." However, understanding that database look-ups can take a long time, particularly during bad weather when flights are delayed or cancelled, we didn't want a number like "three" to be the first thing callers heard without first providing some context. To get around this, we used the phrase "I found a few flights that match that itinerary." Besides providing context for the flight information to come, it lets the caller know that, although the system thinks it's close to finding the right flight, it's not quite there yet. The system then goes on to say, almost parenthetically, "Three, to be exact." This serves to inform the caller of the scope of the work they will be undertaking.

The next part of the prompt—"Help me find the right flight"—is an example of reciprocity, as discussed in Chapter 3. It tells the caller that, although the system wants to get them the right information, the caller needs to do a little more work to narrow down the search, and it motivates the caller to do the work.

The final phrase—"Here's the first one on my list"—is spoken quite quickly, for two reasons; we want to get to the information fast, and we want callers to feel that it will be easy. It reminds me of what happens when a small child trips and falls. The child will look up as if to ask, "Should I cry?" If our faces show alarm, the child will definitely cry. But if we smile and reassure the child that no serious harm has been done, the kid will happily resume playing. Similarly, we want a caller to feel that this will be a quick and easy task.

CONTINENTAL AIRLINES: A DIFFERENT APPROACH TO FLIGHT INFORMATION

Like United Airlines, Continental Airlines has a flight information system. But, unlike the United system, the Continental application asks the user, "Do you know the flight number?" immediately after identifying itself.

The Continental clients chose this design because they wanted to get people interacting with the speech application in an easy, comfortable way. The system then collects the flight number or, if the caller doesn't know the number, the itinerary. Although the application doesn't say so, callers can respond to the first prompt ("Do you know the flight number?") by saying, "Yes, flight 245"—a very conversational and natural response.

The differences between the United and Continental systems reflect several factors: Different people designed them; they have different calling populations; and each one was designed to reflect its company's brand. Although they work differently, they work equally well. Above all, they prove that there is no single, perfect design for any given application; there can, in fact, be many effective ways to achieve the same goal.

A TOP-FIVE INVESTMENT MANAGEMENT COMPANY: HANDLING COMPLEX TWO-CHOICE QUESTIONS

Whenever possible, speech-recognition system designers try to keep prompt questions simple—"Would you like the red, yellow, or green car?" or "What should we change—the time, date, or amount?" However, there are times when the questions are unavoidably more complex. Often, the most complex questions ask the caller to choose between two options that need to be described in more than a few words. The following example shows one way to handle these situations.

Like all financial services systems, the investment company's system enables the caller to identify and correct an error before a transaction is executed. After the user has notified the system that something is incorrect, the system *could* reply

> **"Which part was wrong—the month that you wanted the automatic payment to stop, or the month that you wanted the automatic payment to resume?"**

It sounds like a reasonable and easy to understand question, doesn't it? The problem is that callers wouldn't know how to respond. Do they say, "The month that I want it to resume," "the resuming month," or perhaps just the word "resume?"

The designer of the system solved this problem by collapsing the language structure of the question, making it easier for callers to know how to respond.

> **"Which month was wrong—the stopping month or the resuming month?"**

This works because the context of "automatic payment" has already been established in a prior statement (callers are, after all, changing something they have already identified as incorrect).

AN ONLINE BROKERAGE FIRM:
MANAGING MORE COMPLEX TASKS

There are also times when changing the language is not enough. In this example, we wanted to ask callers how they would like to change their preferences, but the language got unwieldy.

> "Would you like to have me change your preferences so that they are played at the beginning of every call, or change them so that they're played only at the beginning of the first call you make to the system each day?"

That's a mouthful—and few (if any) callers would know how to respond to it. However, there is a simple technique to resolve this situation. The format is

> "I can do [complex task a] or [complex task b]. Would you like me to do [abbreviated task a]?"

By following this format, callers hear the first option, then the second option, and while the second option is still fresh in their minds, they hear a quick reminder of the first task, and then simply answer a yes or no question.

> "I can change your preferences so that they're played at the beginning of every call, or I can just play your preferences once a day, during the first call. Should I play them each time you call in—yes or no?"

This approach reduces the cognitive load on callers and they don't have to learn a long command they may never use again.

AN ONLINE BROKERAGE FIRM: PREFERENCES
AND OTHER RARELY USED FUNCTIONS

Designers are often tempted to make every menu a list of options or commands, particularly when there are four to six items from which to choose. However, if callers are in part of an application they may use only once in a while, we don't want them to have to think about remembering a lot of commands.

Often applications have a **preferences section**, in which users can change some settings of how the application works. In a Web browser the preferences section would allow the user to change the default home page. In a speech system the preferences section might allow users to change things like their PIN numbers, how the system provides certain types of information, and so on. Since users seldom need to access the preferences section of an application, they won't have the opportunity to learn the commands of the possible choices. A bad example of how a prompt for a preferences section would be

> "Would you like to change 'How I read stock information,' 'How verbose the
> prompts are,' 'Your PIN number,' or 'Your personal information?'"

A better alternative is to walk callers through a process that is slightly longer but does not require them to learn a single command. It also saves designers from having to write extremely compact commands. Here's how it works.

SYSTEM: Preferences. Would you like to change how I read the stock information? Yes
or no?

CALLER: *No.*

SYSTEM: OK. Change how long the prompts are?

CALLER: *No.*

SYSTEM: OK. Change your PIN number?

CALLER: *Yes.*

SYSTEM: Got it. Let's get your new PIN number. <System collects new PIN number>
And that will be the new PIN you'll use whenever you call in. Back to

> preferences: Would you like to change the personal information I have on file for you?
>
> CALLER: *No.*
>
> SYSTEM: OK, that was the last preference. Main menu ....

Reducing everything to a "yes or no" question makes the interaction much easier for both the designer and the caller. This method is particularly useful in parts of the application that are less frequently used and when the options in question don't form a cohesive group.

A REGIONAL TELEPHONE COMPANY: DEALING WITH LEGAL NOTICES AND DISCLAIMERS

Have you ever heard a radio commercial for a car dealer in which the announcer speed-reads the financing terms and conditions in the final five seconds? Like the fine print in a newspaper ad, that information has to be there by law—never mind that no listener can actually understand what's being said!

Many speech-recognition applications also require legal disclaimers or notices to be read to callers at some point—usually to protect the client from liability. Legal language needs to be precise, but a good lawyer should be able to make the statement simple and clear without using any confusing or arcane legal terminology. After all, the point is to have lay people understand the terms and conditions of the application. A lawyer will also be able to tell the designer the conditions under which the disclaimer must be played, so that the designer can incorporate this text at the right points in the application and can determine if a disclaimer may or may not allow the caller to interrupt the prompt.

The downside of including a legal notice in an application is that it can be disruptive, user-unfriendly, and time-consuming. I found that out for myself not long ago when I signed up for voice mail from my local telephone company. Immediately after I dialed in for the first time, the system launched—actually, exploded is a better word—into a stream of poorly written legal text that ran about two minutes. I was required to listen to the whole thing and then press "1" to accept the terms and conditions before I could even learn about my voice mail account.

Could this have been handled in a more palatable way? Yes. The voice on the system should have first introduced the subject by saying that it was about to read a required legal statement about the terms and conditions of using the voice mail system. It should have prefaced the statement by summarizing its purpose in simple language. And it should have informed me about how long it would take. A better approach might be:

> **"OK, before we get going I have to read the official terms and conditions of using this system. Basically, it will tell you about how [the phone company] isn't liable in the event that technical failures make it impossible for us to retrieve particular voice messages. If you want to learn more about it after I read it, you can press 'zero' and talk to an operator. OK, here goes—it takes about a minute and a half: 'Whereas the provider of the voice mail service ... <rest of the legal statement>.'"**

After playing the statement, the system should ask callers if they want to hear it again (not that anyone would) or tell them how to accept the terms. The big advantage of this technique is that it doesn't disrupt the collaborative relationship the system is trying to develop with the caller. It simply excuses itself for having to read a statement that is totally inconsistent with the rest of its *personality*.

WILDFIRE: LIST NAVIGATION

Many applications include lists of information through which callers need to navigate, such as lists of voice mail messages, rental car choices, airline flights, and so on. To ensure a positive—and quick—experience for callers, it's important to provide them with easy **list management** directions.

Before informing callers about how to handle list navigation, the system must first tell them:

* That there is a list

* How many items are on it

* And how the system has arranged these items

For example, when Wildfire users call in to check their voice mail or e-mail messages, the system first tells them how many new messages there are, and how it has ordered them: "OK, I've found 15 unread messages and I've ordered them newest first." The nice thing about this method is that the caller can sort them, and then specify the type of sort: "Oldest first," "By priority," "By sender," or even "The other way."

WILDFIRE: SMALL HEADER, LARGE BODY LISTS

The most essential thing about list management is ensuring that the caller feels in control of the list. One way to do this is to let callers hear some information about the first item, and then let them decide if they want to go on to the "Next item," "Previous item," or get more details about the current item. This works particularly well when the information can be presented in a brief "snapshot," as in the following example.

SYSTEM: **Message from "Tim Lawlor."**
CALLER: *Next item.*
SYSTEM: **Message from "Mike Ahnemann."**
CALLER: *What's it say?*
SYSTEM: **Hey Blade, can you give me a call back about the paper? I'll be in the office until 6:00 today. Thanks, bud.**

This is what I call a "small header, large body" list item. Although the **preview** doesn't reveal the actual contents of the message, it does inform the caller of its source, which may provide an important clue about its importance or priority.

A TOP-FIVE U.S. BANK: LARGE HEADER, SMALL BODY LISTS

There are also "large header, small body" list items. For these, it's often better to just broadcast the list to callers and let them interrupt the system when they've found the item they want. Although this forces callers to be paced by the system (rather than allowing them to pace the interaction themselves), this technique can be useful if interesting information is contained in that short description.

For example, a typical banking application might read out a list of transactions to callers, allowing them to interrupt when they want more information. In this situation, the preview information is the bulk of what most callers want to know, as in the following example.

> SYSTEM: OK, I've got all your recent transactions for the past 60 days, ordered newest first. If you want me to stop reading them say "I'm done," and if you want to find out more about one of them say "Describe it." Here goes: An ATM withdrawal, in the amount of $100, was made on July 26th. An automatic withdrawal in the amount of $243.35 was made on July 21st. An ATM withdrawal in the amount of $60 was made on July 12th. A—
>
> CALLER: *(Barges in) Describe it.*
>
> SYSTEM: OK. A withdrawal in the amount of $60 was made from a non–U. S. savings bank, located at <text-to-speech engine reads: "One Financial Center, Boston, Mass.">. The next transaction ….

In this example, the caller gets the bulk of the information in the list item, but has the option to get more information by simply saying a phrase.

THE "RACE CONDITION"

One possible problem with the "large header, small body" technique I've just described deals with a potential lack of synchronicity between the system and the caller—called a

race condition. If a caller isn't quick to say "Describe it" before the system finishes saying an item, the system might incorrectly assume that the caller wants to hear more about the item that follows it. This can be avoided by programming the system to pause between each item or by writing the prompts so that they provide ample time for callers to barge in and hear more about an item. Here's an example of the latter approach.

> SYSTEM: **The next transaction was a deposit of $952.00 on January 29th. The next transaction was ....**

By beginning each item with the phrase "The next transaction was," we give callers enough time to interrupt and say "Describe it" to get more information about the previous item—in this case, the deposit on January 29th.

FEDEX: SCAFFOLDING PROMPTS

FedEx wanted to create a speech-recognition system that would help people in its U.S. market determine how much it would cost to send packages. They knew that people who call them on the phone (that is, don't use the Web interface or a rate book) don't ship frequently. So this application had to work for people with little FedEx shipping experience.

Most people ship packages using the standard FedEx envelopes and boxes. But some use their own packaging. FedEx needed to obtain the dimensions of these nonstandard containers from the callers to ensure that they were not too large to send via the FedEx standard service.

The system was designed to ask each dimension using slightly different text. Here's how the series of questions ran.

> SYSTEM: **OK, what type of package are you shipping? You can say "FedEx letter envelope," "FedEx pack," "FedEx box," "FedEx tube," or you can say "My own packaging."**
>
> CALLER: *My own packaging.*
>
> SYSTEM: **OK. What's the approximate weight of the package in pounds?**

CALLER: *Uh, six pounds.*

SYSTEM: What's the approximate length of your package, in inches? Please round off to the nearest inch.

CALLER: *Eleven inches.*

SYSTEM: OK, what's the approximate width, in inches?

CALLER: *Twelve inches.*

SYSTEM: What's the height?

CALLER: *Eighteen inches.*

This is an example of **scaffolding prompts**. In scaffolding prompts, questions in a series become progressively shorter based on the knowledge callers have gained as they go along. When the FedEx system starts asking about the dimensions of the container, the system incrementally shortens the text with each successive question. This structure assumes—as a "real person" would in similar circumstances—that most people can remember the directions they were given when the questioning began.

In the first question about dimensions, the system asks for the "approximate length" in "inches"—also "rounded off to the nearest inch." This is meant to convey that the exact length isn't important, but the units must be in whole inches (not fractions) and not in centimeters, cubits, or any other unit of measurement.

The next question is a variation of the first one. The system asks for the approximate "width" of the container, but again reminds the caller to measure in inches. Why the reminder? Because a caller might say a package is 18 inches long and 2 feet wide. We don't want them to forget that we're looking only for responses in inches.

Now, after asking the caller two similar questions, and receiving two valid answers (as far as the recognizer is concerned), we can assume the caller has the hang of things. Therefore, we can make the final question brief and casual—"What's the height?"

Callers appreciate the scaffolding prompt structure, not only because it spares them from answering unnecessarily lengthy questions, but also because it is what they would expect in a conversation with a real person.

So what happens if the caller has problems with the second question? As data taken from the FedEx system (and others) show, callers seldom have problems knowing how to answer the subsequent, similar question. But even for the ones who do have problems, the timeout and retry prompts help them answer the question by providing an example or telling them how to use touchtones to enter the information.

In the FedEx Rate Finder system, the system first asks for the length, then width, and then height. If the caller gets to the second question (for the width) and for some reason doesn't know how to answer the system, the first timeout prompt tells the caller, "I didn't hear you. Please say the approximate width of your package in inches, and round off to the nearest inch." However, if the caller said something that the system didn't understand, it assumes that the caller was on the right track, but for some reason it couldn't understand the response and says, "Please say the approximate width again, for example, you could say seven inches."

If the caller doesn't respond a second time, then the system plays the second timeout prompt and provides even more information, "Sorry, I didn't hear you that time either. Using the telephone keypad, enter the approximate width of your package in inches. If you need help, just say 'Help.'" Whereas if the caller says something again that the system doesn't understand, it plays the second retry prompt that was designed to assume that the conditions of the call might have changed to make recognition difficult (after so many successful interactions with the system that has lead them here) and tells the caller, "Please enter the approximate width, in inches, using the telephone keypad."

The point here is to understand that every caller must go through the entire sequence—from step 1 to step 2 to step 3—and generally, the majority will learn along the way. Once the context has been established, the system need only prompt them with as much information as necessary to answer each question.

AMTRAK: IMPLICIT CONFIRMATION AND THE "ELLIPSES/AND" QUESTION FORM

The "ellipses/and" ("... and") form of question is a quick and effective way to ask callers a series of two or more related questions. For example, when people want to get a train's status from Amtrak, they first have to indicate if they want arrival or departure information, and then say the departure and arrival train stations. Here's how a typical call goes.

SYSTEM: Would you like arrival or departure information?

CALLER: *Arrival.*

SYSTEM: What station is the train arriving in?

CALLER: *New York Penn Station.*

SYSTEM: ... and what's the departure station?

In this example, the system asks for the arrival station first because the caller is seeking arrival information. And since the caller understands that the system also needs to collect the location of the departure station, it's more natural for the system to treat it as a two-part question using the ellipses/and form ("... and what's the departure station?") rather than the more formal, parallel question, "What station is the train departing from?"

The ellipses/and form can be used in almost all contexts where the caller is being asked to answer a series of related questions, as in the following two examples.

SYSTEM: OK, what's the make of the car?

CALLER: *Porsche.*

SYSTEM: ... and the model?

CALLER: *Nine forty-four.*

SYSTEM: What's the street address?

CALLER: *695 Atlantic Avenue.*

SYSTEM: ... and the zip code?

CALLER: *02114.*

AIRTRAN: REDUCING THE INFORMATION BURDEN

The AirTran flight information system is different from the United and Continental systems because AirTran serves fewer cities than the other two airlines do. This enables the designer to optimize how the system filters data. When a caller doesn't know the flight number, the system asks for the flight itinerary.

SYSTEM: ... and the originally scheduled departure time? If you're not sure say "I don't know."

CALLER: *I don't know.*

SYSTEM: **All right, but if you had to guess, is it departing in the morning, afternoon, evening, or night?**

Since AirTran doesn't offer multiple flights within the same time block, the system can reduce the burden on the user to know the exact time or even the approximate hour. All they need to know is the general time of day.

GUESSING RIGHT

Sometimes applications need to anticipate the unspoken needs of the users. In the AirTran system, the database has been designed to conduct flight arrival and departure information searches not only for the cities AirTran serves, but also for the cities it doesn't fly to.

SYSTEM: **Great, what's the arrival city?**

CALLER: *Norfolk, Virginia.*

SYSTEM: **I'm sorry, but AirTran doesn't currently serve Norfolk, Virginia. However, AirTran does fly to the Newport News-Williamsburg International Airport in Newport News, Virginia—which is relatively close by. Do you want me to check for flights at that city?**

Because the database can check the proximity of non-AirTran cities to airports that AirTran does serve, it can anticipate callers' desires.

SEMANTICS: WHEN "PROBLEM" WAS A PROBLEM

Once, while designing a large mail-order system, I wrote the following prompt: "You can say 'Place an order,' 'Check inventory,' or 'Report a problem.'" The client didn't like the prompt because they didn't want to use the word "problem." They said their legal staff would reject it, because they never allowed them to use the word "problem" in any literature, or in the spoken words of any customer care representative, at any time.

This was a problem for me.

They suggested that I use "Question about a product." It was now my obligation to disagree with the client. Suppose I buy a new television set, plug it into the wall, and it starts to smoke. I don't have a "question about a product"—I have a "problem with a product!" I don't want an *answer;* I want *resolution.*

The client was also worried that the use of the word "problem" might cause customers to become concerned about the quality of their products. This notion was a little funny to me, because this phone line was being set up to handle, among other things, calls from people who had problems. I told them I understood their concern. Then I explained my other reasons for wanting to use the word.

I believe that if a company *says* the word "problem" in the right way and in the right context, they are not suggesting that they have lots of them. In fact, it might be comforting to a customer without problems to know that there's a line set up to help them should they encounter one. For that matter, if a caller ever encounters a problem, they'll be less likely to call into the system and automatically press "zero" to get to an operator. They'll know that the system can help them.

Besides, everyone knows that all people and companies make mistakes. It's not *making* a mistake that sours the public on a company's brand; it's how the company *reacts to* the mistake. If it resolves the problem promptly and courteously, it can actually cause customers to think better of the company than they did before they ever had a problem!

I've often heard people say, "I don't mind paying a little more at Store X, because if there's a problem, there *is no* problem." These customers know that when issues arise, they'll get resolution quickly and easily. Good companies know that getting another chance to get in *touch* with a customer—for whatever reason—can be an opportunity to improve their relationship with them.

I explained all of these points to the client and the company's legal department. I also pointed out that using the word "problem"—a word that callers are more likely to generate spontaneously—would actually help the system's performance and ensure a faster, more satisfactory resolution.

After much discussion, they relented. "Problem" was allowed—but only in this one system.

WHERE WE'VE BEEN—WHERE WE MUST GO

The only way to improve as a designer is to design—a lot. As the number of speech-recognition applications multiply, some styles will emerge as standards. We've already begun to see that happen with particular commands and phrases. However, great designers—iconoclasts—will know when to break these standard conventions (because they know them so well), producing new ones that will capitalize on both our instincts as humans as well as the common parlance of their society.

Examine things that are seemingly disparate from speech interfaces so that you can learn the underpinnings of how other people communicate in other ways. Learn about sign language to understand a language that has radically different syntax, examine painting to understand how the idea of rhythm is expressed without sound, examine how other people criticize things you love, to learn why they've come to their conclusions, then design. Design a lot.

When we talk about conveying ideas in speech-recognition systems, we tend to think of spoken prompts and responses. But spoken words are not the only way to share ideas. We can convey complex ideas aurally without speaking a single word. Dmitri Shostakovitch proved that in 1937 when he premiered his Fifth Symphony (Op. 47).

Shostakovitch lived in Stalinist Russia—a time of violent oppression when dissidents and perceived rivals were either eliminated by the secret police or shipped off to labor camps in Siberia. The Soviet government only tolerated those artists and writers whose work reflected Stalinist views and Socialist Realism orthodoxy.

Like many of his fellow citizens, Shostakovitch was horrified by the regime's brutality and its efforts to quash free speech—and he was determined to express his opinions through his music. Accordingly, he wrote the finale of the Fifth Symphony with two musical themes that played independently as well as together. One theme is melodic and sorrowful; the other is driven by relentless, pounding drums and the shrill repetition of an "A" note.

After the premiere performance in Leningrad, the audience reaction was overwhelming. They stood and cheered for over an hour, then ran through the streets to share their excitement with others. The audience clearly understood that the first theme represented the suffering of the people, and the second theme represented the iron fist of Stalinist oppression, in cellist Mstislav Rostropovich's words, "like a spear point jabbing in the wounds of a person on the rack." One person in the audience said, "After the first movement we looked around rather nervously, wondering whether we might be arrested after the concert." Not a single word was spoken, but everyone understood the message. Everyone, that is, except the government censors. Fortunately for Shostakovich, they interpreted the finale as representing the triumph of Communism.

Other conductors have also, seemingly, missed the meaning of the finale of the Fifth Symphony. For example, in a recording by Leonard Bernstein and the New York Philharmonic, the pounding tympanis sound more like the triumphant finale of a 1950s musical than the crushing of a nation's spirit.

Besides demonstrating the power of nonverbal communication, this story makes three important points about conveying ideas—no matter what the medium is. To be successful in conveying an idea:

* The communicator needs to know the intended audience

* The recipient of the communication needs to be part of that intended audience

* The communication's vehicle needs to adhere to the intent of the communicator

It's as true for a speech-recognition system as it is for a symphony. We must keep our audience's needs foremost in our minds. We must be consistent with every element of the production of the design to ensure that all the meaning is conveyed—clearly, quickly, and unambiguously. We must ensure that every word expressing every idea has a reason to be there, and that every sound enhances the meaning of those ideas.

If we know our audience well and remain true to our clients' intent from start to finish, we will be successful in conveying our ideas and meeting all the needs of our audience.

SUGGESTED READING LIST

This list is arranged to follow the organization of the chapters, starting with psychology and researching, then going on to hit the topics of designing, writing, producing, branding, usability, deployment, and art.

The Media Equation: How People Treat Computers, Television, and New Media Like Real People and Places by Byron Reeves and Clifford Nass (New York: Cambridge University Press, 1996)

This book is the standard for understanding how people work with technologies on a psychological level. It provides concrete insights into how we can take advantage of the social-psychological interaction between callers and computers.

Things That Make Us Smart: Defending Human Attributes in the Age of the Machine by Donald A. Norman (Reading, MA: Addison-Wesley, 1994)

In addition to Norman's other great work, this book helps the reader understand how to think about taking a human-centered view of not just how to make better designs, but also how to think about determining which tasks are best to automate.

Film Directing Shot by Shot: Visualizing from Concept to Screen by Steven D. Katz (Studio City, CA: Wiese Productions, 1990)

The relevant ideas contained in this book are the similarities between film and speech-recognition systems. Read this book with a view to understanding the semi-linear nature of these two experiences, the method of visualizing the story (storyboarding as an analog to vision clips), and the structure of the production schedule.

The Synonym Finder by J. I. Rodale (New York City: Warner Books, 1986)

Designers for speech systems are surrounded by words and often find that it's hard to uncover just the right word to express an idea (perhaps to soften or strengthen it), or to find a different word to use in a particular context to avoid repetition. This text provides an easy and fast way to locate those words.

A New Brand World: Eight Principles for Achieving Brand Leadership in the 21st Century by Scott Bedbury and Stephen Fenichell (New York City: Viking Penguin, 2002)

Read this book to gain understanding into how particular companies build brands well, and to learn about the role that brands play in the larger corporate environment.

Usability Engineering by Jakob Nielsen (San Francisco, CA: Morgan Kaufmann Publishers, 1994)

Nielsen sets the standard for understanding the details of conducting usability tests in this easy-to-read, comprehensive work.

Design Paradigms: Case Histories of Error and Judgment in Engineering by Henry Petroski (New York City: Cambridge University Press, 1994)

This book takes an interesting approach on gaining insight into designs by analyzing historical design failures. As with usability testing and deploying a system, the postmortem analysis of failures gives insight into how we can establish better design processes.

Theories of Modern Art: A Source Book by Artists and Critics by Herschel B. Chipp (Berkeley: University of California Press, 1984)

Chipp's book is the standard for understanding how people think and talk about art in a modern context. While not accessible to all, use this book to gain understanding into the basic theories of modern art so that you can examine, chronologically, the radical movements in the art world and then apply the same underlying concepts to producing new interface designs.

All these terms are defined in the context of over-the-phone speech-recognition applications.

Audio file   Digital sound file that the computer plays to a caller.

Audio icon   A short, sometimes musical, sound.

Back end   A database that provides information to a speech application.

Branding   The process of embodying aspects of a company's corporate identity.

Call flow   The structure of how the system branches based on the callers' responses.

Call scripts   A list of prompts to be recorded by a voice talent.

Concatenative TTS   A form of text-to-speech that splices pieces of prerecorded human speech.

Confirmation prompt   A type of prompt used to verify that the system correctly understood the caller.

Down sampling   The process of converting high-fidelity recordings into low-fidelity ones, mimicking the sound quality of a typical telephone line.

Failure prompt   A type of prompt used to indicate that the system has failed to help the caller, either due to the lack of caller responses or lack of responses that are "understood" by the recognizer.

Formant TTS   A form of text-to-speech that uses a noise generator and a series of filters to change the noise to make it sound like speech.

Front end   Another name for the speech-recognition application/system.

Full deployment   The last stage of deployment, where the system takes 100% of the intended call volume.

Help prompt   A prompt used to provide more information to a caller, enabling them to better understand how to use the system.

Initial prompt   The first prompt that is played when in a particular state/context.

Morphological analysis   A comparison of similar designs.

Partial deployment   The second stage of deployment, used to examine how the technical performance of the system performs under real-world conditions.

Pilot test   The first stage of deployment, used to examine the user-interface performance.

Quality assurance test   A test performed to ensure that the application performs according to the specification.

Recognition engine/Recognizer   The technology that listens to audio and then compares it to a set of known patterns.

Recoverable error   An error that can be rectified by the user.

Retry prompt   A prompt used to provide the caller assistance when the system has detected human speech but does not understand it.

Speaker-dependent recognizer   A recognizer that only works for a particular person and must be tuned by listening to a person saying known phrases.

Speaker-independent recognizer   A recognizer that performs equally well for a large segment of the population.

Speaker verification   Technology used to match the biometrics of a person's voice to a known voiceprint, primarily used for authentication.

Speech scientist   A person who can, among other things, tune a recognizer to perform better based on a statistical analysis of the recognizer's performance.

State   A context of the dialogue, typically where the system asks a question and listens for an answer. Also called a **turn**.

Success prompt   A prompt that indicates a user is about to progress to the next state, having completed the state they are in.

Telephony-based speech recognition   Recognition performed by a computer listening to speech over a phone line.

Text-to-speech (TTS) Technology that converts text stored in a digital form to a spoken utterance, in real time.

Timeout prompt A prompt used to provide the caller assistance when the system has not detected any sound above a (low) threshold.

Turn A context of the dialogue, typically where the system asks a question and listens for an answer. Also called a **state**.

Unrecoverable error An error that cannot be rectified by the user.

Usability test A test used to determine the quality of the user interface, typically run with a few people in a controlled environment.

Vision clip An audio file that sounds like a recorded conversation between a speech-recognition system and a caller, typically used to illustrate the design of a not-yet built system.

Voice talent A person hired to speak phrases.

INDEX